Lindsay, at long last!

Bastarᴆ
Яepцƃɩic

Encounters Along the Tattered
Edge of Fallen Empire

Thanks for your excellent work!

Tyrine

6/5/17

Acclaim for Tyrone Shaw's

Bastard Republic

"*Bastard Republic* is a thrilling ride. It had me in its clutches from the first page and didn't let go until the last. Here is literary journalism of the highest order—informative, compelling, and utterly readable. Masterfully combining historical events, personal narrative, and the keenly-observed changing political climate of post-Soviet era Eastern Europe, this book is a marvel."

Jensen Beach, author of *Swallowed by the Cold*

"Tyrone Shaw's *Bastard Republic* is a raconteur's blend of reportage and cultural anthropology. This is not a breezy, drive-through travelogue. Shaw knows his territory intimately. Through richly textured scenes and brilliant exposition, he brings alive the painful contradictions that define this troubled and troubling eastern flank of Europe."

Tony Whedon, author of *A Language Dark Enough*

"Why is the individual perspective so compelling, and even necessary, when deconstructing world history? Because how else to know the human, personal consequences when superpowers run roughshod over the people they control? Shaw, as a journalist, does more than merely cover the tragic history of Moldova. His personal narrative intersects with global events of epic proportions. This stunning and important book is a lesson in world history as well as a tale about what happens to the human heart when it struggles against power run amok."

Sue William Silverman, author of *The Pat Boone Fan Club: My Life as a White Anglo-Saxon Jew*

Bastard Яepџблıc

Encounters Along the Tattered
Edge of Fallen Empire

Tyrone Shaw

ISBN: 978-0-692-82669-0
Printed in the United States of America.
Cover photos, front and back, by Nicolae Pojoga
Some of the chapters in this book appeared in modified form in *Green Mountains Review, Sararanc Review*, and *The Truth about the Fact*.

The names of Ghennady and Natalia Sokolov and Oleg Serov have been changed for their protection.

Published by Lost Nation Books

For Nicolae Pojoga

ACKNOWLEDGMENTS

The author would like to thank the following:

Emily Copeland, for her keen editorial insight and dedication to this project; Alyssa Barrett, for her laser-like proofreading eye; Lindsay Francescutti, for her work designing this edition; Sue William Silverman, for abundant encouragement and guidance during this book's inception; Nancy Shaw, for generous, honest feedback and her acceptance of my sometimes ill-advised curiosity; Johnson State College, for its crucial financial support, which made many of the trips chronicled in this book possible; and Ralph Rosenberg—physician, philosopher, artist, and dear friend—for his steadfast belief that *Bastard Republic* should be published.

CONTENTS

PREFACE

Chişinău, Moldova, March 2014

A cold drizzle coats us as we huddle around a fire in Lica Sainciuc's front yard in Chişinău, the capital of the Republic of Moldova. Lica was born in this rambling stone, wood, and stucco single-story house with a vegetable garden, grape vines, and plum trees, but in another country—the Soviet Union. His father, Glebus, was born here too, in yet a different nation—Romania—almost a century ago. And his grandfather built this place in what was then another country still—imperial Russia. His squat, solid house has, like its residents, endured a fraught history of empires gained and lost.

Yet Russia remains close by, not in terms of miles, but in the head and heart. It is for many Moldovans the devil they know best, oppressive but familiar, like an abusive parent. Neighboring Ukraine is beginning to unravel, and the Russians are coming again. At least that is the palpable fear and is mostly why we are all getting drunk tonight in the classic Moldovan style: repeated glasses of strong homemade brandy to accompany costiţă—spicy grilled pork—and pickled vegetables. This is, my old friend Nicolae Pojoga tells me, the only sane way to cope with Russian aggression. "Yes," he says as he carefully turns the meat over the coals, "in this way, we protest heroically!" His logic is sound: better drunk than dead. Everyone here knows what happens when the Russians decide to meddle.

As if anyone needs further reminding of that, Pojoga, who is a former Soviet war photographer and is now a prominent Moldovan photojournalist and photographer, will host an exhibition tomorrow at the Brancusi Center of sixty-two of his now-iconic photographs documenting the civil war that partitioned the new nation in 1992 and left several thousand Russian peacekeeping forces in the break-away region of Transnistria. The event, sponsored by the Moldovan Interior Ministry, is designed to commemorate the victims of that brief but bloody conflict. On a much larger scale, perhaps, a similar fate may well now await neighboring Ukraine.

As he looks up from the fire, I am struck by how little Nicolae has changed over the years I have known him. His features remain sharply defined: a narrow hawk-like nose divides his gaunt, angular face. A close-cropped gray beard softens the lines somewhat. He would appear menacing, perhaps, were it not for his extraordinary hazel eyes. They are probing yet disarmingly kind.

Eventually the rain and cold drive us inside into the small, brightly lit kitchen where we watch a televised invasion by stealth. What are obviously Russian troops have taken control of much of Crimea's capital, Sevastapol, and Crimea—part of Ukraine only since 1954—seems destined to return to Mother Russia.

"This could get *very* interesting," says Sandor Canţîr, a former longtime correspondent for BBC and longtime friend, as he fills my glass again.

My work conducting ethics seminars for university journalism students and collaborating with local journalists has allowed me to make good friends here in Chişinău over the years. In some ways, little has changed since my first visit sixteen years ago. Moldova remains Europe's poorest country; it is still tied to Moscow on multiple levels, however ambivalently; and it continues what has been a slow crawl towards the European Union. In one respect, however, things might soon be different. To Moscow's great displeasure, Moldova signed a free-trade agreement with the EU. It is the same agreement that the former president of Ukraine, Viktor Yanukovych, rejected—a decision that sparked a revolution and forced him from office. As part of that agreement, Moldova for the first time will gain access to Europe's markets, and her citizens will not require visas to enter European Union nations, a hugely important symbol towards ending this country's isolation from the West.

Despite that possibility, the mood is grim tonight and the humor mordant. As the Russians seize Crimea, apparently with the whole-sale approval of the Crimeans, I think of another old friend, Evghenia Amambaeva, an ethnic Russian Moldovan. During my first visit to Chişinău in 1998, struck by Moldova's agricultural richness, its highly educated population, its temperate climate, and no doubt under the influence of the country's extraordinary brandy, I bet her $100 that in ten years Moldova would be another Switzerland—a tiny, exquisitely functional nation. The suggestion prompted a raised eyebrow, a snorting laugh, and then a firm handshake.

In 2008, after returning from my sixth visit to Moldova, I wired $100 to Moscow, where Evghenia had fled back to her family, back to her people. I have not heard from her since.

I am often asked why I spend time in the so-called frozen con-flict zone of Transnistria and in other parts of the wreckage of the Soviet Union's sudden implosion in 1991. The response for me is complicated. Curiosity is certainly part of it. As a journalist with a fascination for both history and sociology, the story of this part of the world is irresistible to me. I also *like* these places, where so much has been broken and so much remains to be fixed. I like their exis-tential weirdness, their complexity, their hope, and their despair. More than anything, though, there is a desire to bear witness in some meaningful way to perhaps the biggest story of my time: the collapse of Communism in Eastern Europe and the self-inflicted death of the USSR—the defining bogeyman of my youth. I am in Lica Sainciuc's kitchen tonight chasing the tail of an extinct comet, still harboring a deep regret that I never managed to visit what had been for me growing up a source of lurid, terrifying, and nearly erotic fascination.

The Soviet Union, which President Ronald Reagan referred to as the Evil Empire, was for me in my youth during the height of the Cold War in the 1950s the ultimate existential threat. Its epic menace was deeply imprinted on my brain. Across the country, millions of us schoolchildren were subjected to weekly civil defense drills and the "duck and cover" exercises that required crawling under our little desks and covering our heads with our arms. Running through my confused and vaguely terrified young mind—as the smell of floor wax oozed from the battered oak flooring just inches from my nose—was an absurd nursery rhyme designed to calm our fears of impending annihilation at the hands of the diabolical Soviet Union.

There was a turtle by the name of Bert,
And Bert the Turtle was very alert.
When danger threatened him he never got hurt.
He knew just what to do:
He'd Duck and Cover, Duck and Cover.
He did what we all must learn to do. You and you and you and you!
Duck and Cover!

At the same time, tens of thousands of Americans built bomb shelters and stocked them, they imagined, with enough canned sausages, tuna, potatoes, and beets to get them through the apocalypse. A neighbor had a shelter, its heavy iron door looming mysteriously in his backyard. I asked my father why we didn't have one. "For chrissakes," he said. "Why would anyone even *want* to live in the kind of world we'd have after that?"

I remember the Soviet Union's brutal response to the doomed 1956 Hungarian revolution, mostly through newsreels and *Life* magazine, one picture from which remains indelible in my mind: passersby spitting on the pantless corpse of a Soviet soldier lying face-down in a gutter.

In 1957, the Soviets launched the world's first satellite, and I realized they could now go anywhere, *anywhere at all*, even right over my own house. It was dark magic.

Four years later, with us still playing catch-up, the Soviets perched the world's first human space traveler, Yuri Gagarin, atop a Vostock I rocket—basically a huge Roman candle—and exploded him into orbit. It was, he would comment later, an "interesting ride."

The mercurial, alternately menacing and avuncular Soviet leader, Nikita Khrushchev, gloated once again, boasting to America, "We will bury you." America quaked, but this odd, unscripted apparition had captured my imagination, and my fear now mingled with fascination. As a nerdish eleven-year-old boy, I closely followed Khrushchev's tour of the US in 1959. He joked with Iowa wheat and corn farmers, wolfed down slabs of barbecue, and playfully jousted with the press. Soon enough, though, he would take political theater in a darker direction as he pounded his shoe on the podium during an angry speech at the UN. "Look!" cried the American press. "This man is a lunatic! With the push of a button he can destroy us all!"

So the doomsday clock ticked on, and for thirteen days in 1962, with Soviet missiles newly installed in Cuba at the request of Fidel Castro, the US and the Soviet Union lurched towards nuclear confrontation.

My childhood was filled with the curiously opaque vocabulary of planetary annihilation: *mutually assured destruction, first strike, kill weight, second strike, fail safe, DEFCOM*. It was a youth shaped by Cold War paranoia that seeped into popular culture and produced its own panoply of movies and literature: *On the Beach* and *Fail Safe* fueled my fears of a nuclear Armageddon while Stanley Kubric's *Dr. Strangelove or How I Learned to Stop Worrying and Love the Bomb,* provided brilliantly grim comic relief. I devoured spy thrillers like Graham Greene's *The Third Man*, Ian Fleming's *From Russia with Love*, Len Deighton's *The Ipcress File* and John Le Carre's *The Spy Who Came in from the Cold.* Some of these would become unforgettable movies. Orson Welles's portrayal of the murky Harry Lime turned Greene's seminal novel of deceit into a noir classic, and *From Russia with Love* set the gold standard for a decade of East versus West movie mayhem. Who can forget Lotte Lenya's portrayal of the fiendish Rosa Klebb, the sexually predatory East German intelligence officer with a face like a collapsed lung, a taste for beautiful young women with perky breasts, and a preference for sensible black shoes with poison-laced retractable blades in their toes? And of course there was the fight-to-the-death between Sean Connery and the sinister Soviet double agent Robert Shaw in a six-foot-by-six-foot train compartment on the Orient Express: East meets West in a claustrophobic dance of death, punctuated only by savage grunts and the sound of the carriage wheels rattling on the rails underneath. Twisted loyalties, triple crosses, cloaked motives, and a vast swamp of moral ambiguity tugged at my imagination.

But this roiling East versus West universe would vanish by 1991, beginning with the collapse of Communism in the satellite nations bordering the Soviet Union and ending with the implosion of the USSR itself. The process accelerated with the advent of Soviet reformer Mikhail Gorbachev in 1985 and his policies of *glasnost* (openness) and *perestroika* (restructuring). Three years later, Gorbachev essentially lifted the Soviet yoke from the satellite nations of Poland, East Germany, Hungary, Czechoslovakia, Romania, Bulgaria, and Albania by telling the world they could go their own way. Sensing the collapse of the long-established reality that had shaped so many of my perceptions, I visited Romania in 1988. By then, it was absolutely the most repressive Communist country in Eastern Europe. There, at least, the word *Stalinesque* still rang true, and I expected to experience at long last that vanishing world.

Much of my subsequent travels throughout the edges of what had been one of the two great superpowers of the twentieth century have been driven by a single, central question: what is it like to live here in times of such rough transformation? There is, I think, value in learning the answer and in telling a story that unfolds still.

And so, twenty-six years later, I sit in a snug kitchen in the former Soviet Union surrounded by friends watching television as well-equipped soldiers devoid of identifying insignias take up positions outside government buildings calmly, precisely, and expertly. These people are not amateurs.

"Fucking Russians," says Nicolae.

CITY OF HOPE,
CITY OF FEAR

Bucharest, Romania, February 1990

Badly photographed travel posters featuring boxy high-rise hotels and Gerovital, a strange Romanian pharmaceutical reportedly derived from extracts of monkey glands, greet me as I step into the dark and freezing passenger terminal at Otopeni Airport. Tanks and anti-aircraft batteries loom just beyond the runway, and soldiers flank the soot-streaked glass entrance doors. But here inside, less than six weeks after the bloody overthrow and execution of Romanian leader Nicolae Ceaușescu and his wife, there is an almost punch-drunk energy.

"Welcome to Free Romania," says a smiling customs agent following a cursory inspection of my one duffel bag and my camera case. The spirit of nascent capitalism is evident as I run a gauntlet of cab drivers on my way to the doors leading outside. They grab my arms.

"Forty dollars, good ride!"

"Bucharest, only thirty dollars!"

"Twenty-five!" screams another. I continue walking to a bus idling beside the terminal. As in Ceaușescu times, it will take me eventually to the center of Bucharest for the equivalent of ten cents.

I take a seat at the front of the freezing bus, exhaustion settling in, and I doze for a few minutes until the old bus's diesel growls to life. Fumes from the wheezing engine are sucked in through a hole in the floor somewhere in the vicinity of my seat as we lurch away from the terminal. Across the aisle, an elderly couple crams three suitcases in the luggage rack above the seats. We are the only passengers. The driver, clad in a heavy dark gray coat, lights a Carpaţi, coughs, and roughly grinds the gears. The feeble headlights barely penetrate the soupy fog as we approach the airport exit. Suddenly the hulking shapes of at least a dozen tanks materialize, standing ready, long guns unsheathed to the elements, plumes of exhaust pouring from underneath them.

"What are the tanks there for?" I ask the driver.

He shrugs. "Everybody's nervous right now," he says. "Anything could happen. Maybe the Russians will attack us now that we've thrown the Communists out. Maybe the *Securitate*. Who knows?"

We ride in silence, and I fight to stay awake. Through the streaked windows I cannot see much. Except for the tanks, things look the same as they did eighteen months earlier. But that had been a very different kind of trip, a vacation prompted by a small-town journalist's curiosity to glimpse life in the last of the hard-line Communist regimes in Europe.

No garish neon strip announces our arrival into this sepulchral city, no McDonald's, Pizza Hut, Texaco stations, no expressways with complex clover leaf overpasses. Instead, a potholed two-lane road takes us to the center of a morose, faded capital once known as the Paris of the East. The transition from the countryside is imperceptible at night, and even as we pull into the heart of the city, I see few pedestrians and even fewer cars. It feels like a city under siege.

Lacking functioning streetlights and neon signs, Romania's capital has a vaporous, miasmic unreality: it remains a phantom metropolis. Thick, lignite-fed mist has settled over its center as I leave the bus in University Square. I am now very cold although I have a decent coat. It's a damp, nasty cold that penetrates, a river cold that settles into the bones and clings. Through the fog, the eerie glow of candles punctuates the darkness by the university, marking the spots where so many recently have been killed.

Disoriented by the fog, the darkness and jet lag, I have trouble finding the Union Hotel, which I know is tucked away somewhere nearby in a narrow street. Having been warned of the vagaries of securing winter hotel accommodations in Bucharest in the fighting's aftermath, I booked a few nights at this modest hotel through a travel agency specializing in the Eastern Bloc.

Troops, tanks and personnel carriers ring the square as I pass by the university. Small groups of soldiers lean against buildings, smoking nervously and talking quietly among themselves. In the middle of the nearly deserted square, a group of young men and women—students probably—form a semicircle around a makeshift shrine marking the spot where a friend or family member had been killed in December. In perfect harmony, they sing an old Orthodox hymn while holding flickering votive candles. The cold, mingling with the sharp smell of burning wax, stings my nose, but I am captivated by the brittle melancholy of the voices. I stop and listen, the young faces dimly illuminated by the candles. After a few minutes, a policeman walks by and he too stops. He stands and shifts his feet in the cold.

I ask him to point me in the direction of my hotel. "I will take you there," he says. "It's confusing out here in the fog." He walks me across the square and through a warren of side streets to the Union.

"You have a strange accent," he says. "Where are you from?"

"The United States."

"Ah. America," he says wistfully. "I have a cousin in Chicago. Now maybe I will be able to visit him. Maybe I will live there myself."

I tell him I hope he gets to visit. I find it strange, at this moment, to think of our two countries—mine where I believe democracy is slowly dying, and his, where perhaps it is just being born.

"Suddenly we have a lot of foreigners now, and that is amazing," he says. "This is like a dream for me. Now I can talk to anyone!"

His behavior, I will discover, is typical, and like almost everyone I will meet in the next two weeks, he wants to talk to anyone from the West, really to anyone who will listen. The country is emerging from decades of silence, and people now seem to want to talk nonstop, to anyone and everyone. Contact with foreigners, which under Ceaușescu was officially regarded as suspicious, is no longer a problem. I find this need to make contact both touching and a little manic. It is as if they believe that if they talk long enough, the silence will never return.

Within five minutes, he stops. "Here, on your left," he says.

In the darkness I see a dimly lit lobby through a glass door. We shake hands like old friends before he walks into the fog, the sound of his boots echoing off the uneven pavement.

Like all but the most expensive hotels in Romania, the Union is rundown and drab. It is ostensibly a "two-star" establishment, but that is, I suppose, all relative. The few chairs in the lobby are threadbare and sagging, the once attractive mosaic-tile floor chipped and filthy. The lobby is also freezing. Behind a paneled counter, the receptionist, a small mustached man with dark pouches beneath beady, rat-like eyes studies me suspiciously.

"Yes?" he snaps.

"I have a reservation," I say.

"Name?"

"Shaw."

"Passport?"

I hand him my passport, and he begins to thumb through the pages, deliberately, slowly. Eventually he hands me my room key. "Third floor," he says curtly. "Be careful on the way up. The stairs have no lighting."

I am sure this man, like all who have been permitted to work in the hotel industry with access to foreigners, is still linked to the secret police and Ceaușescu's vast machine of spying and intimidation. Most likely, he has been paid directly by them, and by now he is probably wondering how long he will have a job. His past employer may not be a plus on his résumé.

I climb the three flights up the darkened stairway to my room, just large enough to accommodate a single bed, a wardrobe, and a tiny desk. The light by the bed boasts one forty-watt bulb, but the room is clean with even a little heat filtering up from wherever the hot water flows. Against one of the taupe plaster walls, a bad color photograph of a beautiful woman in an intricately embroidered peasant dress looks out happily towards the bed. Another, this one of a collective farm, graces the other wall.

Despite my exhaustion, I cannot sleep. Eighteen months ago, the singing in the square, my friendly chat with the cop and the chaos at the airport would have been unthinkable. Although I left the Romanian Socialist Republic believing something dramatic would eventually happen, I did not think I would be returning so soon and under these circumstances.

By September, 1988, Soviet Premier Mikhail Gorbachev's reforms were dramatically transforming the Soviet Union, and the regimes in East Germany, Poland, Czechoslovakia and Hungary were already preparing their countries for a soft landing; even phlegmatic Bulgaria had climbed aboard the train that would soon jettison its Communist cargo. But not Romania, which had banned official Soviet publications like *Pravda,* deeming them far too liberal. All Western magazines were forbidden, and broadcasts from outside the country were heavily jammed. The country seemed hermetically sealed. The Western media ran numerous stories detailing the deteriorating quality of life under the Ceauşescu regime. By their accounts, harsh austerity measures forced people to heavily ration electricity, heat, and food. The dreaded secret police, the Securitate, had become legendary, and half the people were rumored to be spying on the other half. Some said Ceauşescu was suffering the effects of tertiary syphilis and compared his increasingly erratic behavior to another fulsome despot, Uganda's Idi Amin. Others found an even darker analogy to another famous fellow countryman, Dracula. Romania seemed to be dramatically cast in black and white, its tormented people hungry and shivering in the shadow of momentous change that was beginning to sweep through the rest of Eastern Europe.

This time, I have come to see a very different place, seemingly a new country in its birth throes, and to keep a promise. As I lie in this comfortably hard bed, a feeble groan emanating from the radiator, the students' sweet voices echo in my mind. It is a sad lullaby.

The next morning the fog has lifted, and the ravages of December are evident. Directly across from my hotel, an apartment wall is blackened and pockmarked with bullet holes. Most of the windows are blown out and a section of the roof appears to be open to the overcast sky. In the daylight, I easily navigate my way to a corner facing the square by the former headquarters of the Communist Party. Despite all the vivid, dramatic news photos and video feed during the fighting, I am not prepared for what I see.

The elegant and stately Presidential Palace, which also housed the National Museum of Art, has been radically transformed since my last visit. The filigreed wrought iron gate flanking the entrance is now blackened and twisted. Chunks have been blasted from the five sixty-foot Corinthian columns standing between the huge shattered arched windows on the second floor. A section of the delicately sculpted balcony just below the roof is completely missing, its remains spilled in a heap by the main entrance. One wall is blackened. As I stare at the wreckage, a very young soldier on the other side of the iron gate stares back at me. *"Armată uşoară,"* I say, which is a common greeting to soldiers. It means literally "easy army" and conveys a simple wish that military life for the conscript will be easy. He smiles and nods.

I have a visceral sense of the savagery that played out here just before Christmas. Across the square from where I stand, regular army units engaged Securitate forces loyal to Ceauşescu that had holed up in a wing of this building. It was a vicious firefight, and the old palace now offers mute testimony to the fury of the army's guns during those chaotic days of December 21 and 22.

Ceauşescu had grown increasingly distrustful of the army, which was composed largely of conscripts, and with the exception of a small elite anti-terrorist force, he relied on the Securitate for loyalty, enforcement, and protection. Most were thugs, culled from orphanages and raised by the state to be absolutely obedient to Ceauşescu and his family. They were, like Haiti's *Tonton Macoutes*, a private instrument of terror. They owed him everything, and he treated them well.

When their prime benefactor fell from power, much of the military arm of the Securitate fought tenaciously to reinstate him and preserve their institutional privilege. The army, struggling to make do with obsolete equipment, horrible living conditions, and poor pay, had no such loyalties and inevitably they would side with the people as they rose up against a hated tyrant.

No one knows exactly how many died in that spasm of violence, certainly many hundreds, but the damage to the center of the city is plain to see. By far, the most dramatic—and saddest—causality in this square is the Central University Library. Less than two years ago I stood here soaking in the faded belle-époque splendor of this baroque masterpiece. Now, the graceful cupola is shattered along with the roof, most of which has fallen through to the ground floor. The interior has been entirely gutted by fire.

On December 22, in what could only have been an act of horrific malice, Securitate units fired incendiary bombs directly into the library. The fire was successfully contained, but the following night they returned to the poorly protected building and began firing at regular army units in the square below. The soldiers returned fire. During the exchange, the structure once again caught fire.

This time it burned out of control. More than 500,000 books, some very rare, were destroyed. Now much of the elaborately detailed facade above the blown-out windows is blackened and cracked.

In what seems like an amazingly optimistic gesture, scaffolding now rings the lovely hundred-year-old building and crews have begun repairs. Above me workmen in blue clothing dangle from ropes high above the ground. They are attempting to patch large holes in the walls with new blocks of stone that are raised in baskets from the street below. From one of the balcony windows flanked by bullet-scarred columns, an old woman with a red wool headscarf looks out sadly at the square below. The workers here tell me that the building will be completely restored by August for its centenary, but I have my doubts.

Continuing on my morbid morning tour of an urban battle-ground, I stop at the gutted hulk of the former Securitate headquar-ters across the square. Nothing is left of the incongruously graceful building except its white marble façade, now a mass of holes. I can stare right down through the floors to a deep basement twenty feet below the street. Hundreds have reportedly died here during inter-rogations over the past decades, but there is no evidence of that now. Nothing remains to document what went on here, at least nothing I can see. A man dressed in a suit and a long wool overcoat combs through the debris on the cellar floor, poking piles of charred wood with a long stick. I have no idea what he is doing there, and something tells me not to ask.

At the other end of the square looms the empty Communist Party headquarters. The large sign on the roof that had proclaimed *"Trăiască Partidul Comunist Român"* (Long Live the Communist Party of Romania) has been crudely modified. The offending center words have been hacked away and an *ia* has been tacked on, so the sign now proclaims, "Long Live Romania." I notice something else: curiously, aside from a few broken windows and the odd bullet hole, this building from which Ceaușescu and his wife made their aborted escape in a helicopter appears unscathed. This fact will become more important as conspiracy theories evolve regarding what exactly happened during those chaotic days in December.

What *is* clear is that on December 21, as he had done dozens of times during the past twenty-five years, Nicolae Ceaușescu stood on a balcony here to speak at what he thought would be another carefully orchestrated Ceaușescu love-in, despite the awful events in the western Romanian city of Timișoara a few days earlier. There, on December 17, the Securitate and elite army units had fired upon demonstrators protesting the government's efforts to deport László Tőkés, an ethnic Hungarian pastor who had vociferously opposed the government's religious oppression. Official estimates of the death toll were placed at about 150, but rumors of thousands massacred spread throughout the country. The *New York Times* erroneously reported that as many as four thousand people, including many women and children, had been shot by the Securitate forces. By December 19, regular army units in Timișoara had mutinied and openly sided with the demonstrators. Despite a Romanian news blackout, word of those astonishing events reached millions of Romanians through foreign radio services.

Then, on December 21, from this balcony, Ceaușescu blamed those disturbances on "hooligan (*golani*) elements and Hungarian agents." At one point the "Genius of the Carpathians" (one of his favorite official titles) was greeted with a sonic boom of hatred as jeers, boos, and taunts erupted from the crowd below. It was unthinkable, yet there it was, live, on national television. Confused, Ceaușescu retreated inside the building, and soon he and his equally hated wife fled from the roof in a helicopter. Four days later, after their capture and a one-hour trial, both were executed by a military firing squad, a Christmas-day gift to the people of Romania. Elena Ceauşescu's last words were reportedly directed towards one member of the firing squad: "You motherfucker!"

For the crowd below that window, Ceauşescu's confusion must have been like blood to a shark. Demonstrators, students, and workers, emboldened by the hated dictator's desperate departure, stormed the building as Securitate and army units stood by. It was later reported that no units had received orders to intervene.

Inside, over the next few hours, an ad-hoc government, the National Salvation Front, was formed from a motley collection of former party functionaries, dissidents, writers, poets, military men and academics. Appointed as its head was Ion Iliescu, a one-time Ceauşescu Minister of Youth.

After several hours, Iliescu and Army Chief of Staff General Ştefan Guşă appeared together on the balcony to announce that the army supported the revolution and would not fire on the people, an announcement many would later maintain was premature. This news was greeted with euphoria by the crowd below, which by some estimates had grown to a million.

A few miles away, an obscure army major, Mihai Lupoi, had already been on the television to announce that the army was "with the people," a performance that further galvanized the nation; that appearance would soon enough have curious repercussions for him.

This all was powerfully cathartic for a society long accustomed to the stultifying constraints of Ceauşescu and his jailers. It was also, no doubt, dramatic. I imagine the new government piling into cars under the protection of Guşă's troops as they raced to the television station in an army convoy to present themselves formally to a stunned and disbelieving nation. I imagine them breathless and perhaps terrified as they ran upstairs, their pounding feet echoing in the concrete stairwell, grimfaced soldiers in front of and behind what would soon be the new provisional government of Romania.

They assembled in one of the broadcast studios, and many Romanians got their first glimpse of their new leader huddled around a long table with students, army officers, television personnel and other Front members as a firefight raged outside the windows. Hollywood could not have scripted this better. Danger, intrigue, grace under fire, and suspense—it was all there in that small room, a new government forged in the crucible of battle. Or so it seemed. It was, undoubtedly, great television, great drama, especially considering what had passed for television. The highlight of the normal broadcasting day, aside from the obligatory hosannas to the Great Leader, might be a panel discussion on the patriotic applications of chemical fertilizers to boost yields of grain in the next five-year plan.

Far from those patriotic thoughts of future grain yields, the nation watched spellbound as Securitate units attacked the station while army units that had taken up positions around the station with tanks repelled the assault. In another unexplained peculiarity, despite the seeming brutality of the assault, most of the damage sustained was to the buildings *across* from the station. To be sure, the station itself suffered a few direct hits, but the damage compared to the buildings fired upon by the army was slight.

It also seemed strange to some that the elite Securitate units that attacked the station with assault rifles and briefly with helicopters could not disable the transmitter or cut the power to the now self-proclaimed "Free Romania Television."

Fighting on an even larger scale had erupted in the city center as Securitate units emerged from tunnels beneath the Presidential Palace. Eyewitness accounts clearly indicate that, as in Timişoara, men in army uniforms fired upon demonstrators, killing hundreds during those chaotic hours of December 21-22.

Six weeks later on this cold, overcast morning, I am talking with one of those eyewitnesses as we stand in front of a simple cross marking the spot where someone was killed in the fighting. It is next to other carved crosses, some elaborate and some crudely constructed, many draped with wreaths, flags, photos, and roses already wilting in the sharp air. Candles burn constantly at the base of these shrines and the piquant smell of burning wax mingles with diesel fumes and coal dust.

Corneliu Dominescu is immaculately dressed in pressed trousers and a ski parka. He has the clean-cut wholesome openness of a kid from a prairie town in Kansas. A few minutes before, I had seen him kneeling before this cross and asked if I could take his picture. "No problem," he said. Just behind him tacked up on the stone wall of a university building is a sign reading "Oh, Liberty! How many crimes are committed in your name?" Other signs equate the new government with Hitler, Iliescu with Ceaușescu and Stalin.

I ask him about regular army units firing on people in this square. He nods vigorously. "I saw it with my own eyes. Men in army uniforms opened fire on a group of us. I was shot in the arm, and my friend's face was blown off," he tells me.

Other students come up to us with similar stories, but most of them, like Dominescu, insist that those units firing upon the students *must* have been Securitate disguised as regular army. Most genuinely believe in the good intentions of the Romanian army. Probably the truth will never be known, and here in post-revolutionary Bucharest, rumors float in the air as thickly as the dust and exhaust fumes.

An hour later, I stand in front of one of the prime magnets for those rumors, the unfinished Casa Poporului. It was to be both the center of the glorious Romanian government and Ceaușescu's personal residence, one finally worthy of the Genius of the Carpathians. A boulevard six feet wider than the Champs-Élysée runs from here to Piața Unirri, about a mile and a half away. Ostensibly built in "Neo-Classical French style," the huge edifice looks more like an architectural shotgun marriage of Stalin wedding cake and Disney Gothic.

The second largest building in the world, this monstrosity is by any standards remarkable. Floor space: 3,890,000 square feet; height: 470 feet and 12 stories from ground level, with another 300 feet below ground; 1000 rooms, including over 500 offices, two huge and lavish halls, one of which is 230 feet long, 98 feet wide and 60 feet high; two amphitheaters seating several thousand each; and elaborately outfitted guest suites for hundreds.

I am about a hundred yards away trying to capture the scope of this monument to megalomania with a 45mm lens. Even at this distance, I cannot get the whole building in the frame. Watching me change lenses, a man asks me in Romanian where I am from. Hearing my answer, he shifts into perfect English.

"Well, what do you think?" he asks as I ponder the instant artifact in front of me.

"Astonishing," I reply.

"Yes, that's one word for it," he replies, an edge to his voice.

"I am Octave Fulger," he announces gravely as he extends a hand.
He has an earnest, round face framed by a mass of curly dark hair.
Fulger is an employee of the city, the son of an actor in the National
Theater and a pharmacist—by Ceauşescu standards, one of the
lucky ones.

"Do you know what used to be here...for miles? The most beautiful part of this city...the oldest. Many thousands of people were
forced from their homes which were then destroyed, for this." He
turns his head and spits contemptuously onto the sidewalk. "While
millions of us were freezing in our homes with not enough to eat, he
spent a billion dollars to build this obscenity."

Actually, the tab for this modern Versailles has been estimated
by the World Bank at more than three billion thus far, including
demolition and the total construction of his grand Boulevard of the
Victory of Socialism. A quarter of old Bucharest was razed to make
room for the marble-clad Mussolini Modern buildings that flank
the broad avenue. These not entirely ungraceful buildings contain
thousands of apartments that Octave tells me were intended for the
party faithful and the Securitate forces that ensured their survival.
Since December 21, all construction has ceased, and the entire district, including the flagstone boulevard stretching for miles in the
distance, is eerily empty. On the horizon, idle building cranes probe
the leaden winter sky.

"You are looking at the world's most expensive stage set,"
Octave says.

Among the most persistent rumors is that most of the architects
who worked on the initial phase of the design and construction have
disappeared. "They knew too much about the secret tunnels con-
necting this to the center of the city," insists one bystander.

Octave assures me it is true. "That man is right. Even today we
can't find these tunnels," he says.

An old woman shakes her head. Like many people in Bucharest,
she is convinced that an army of Securitate has massed beneath the

city, waiting to ascend from subway stations and manhole covers to wage a war of terror on the populace. "That's because nobody knows where to look, but thousands of them live here now in this building underground, like rats."

The prevalence of this suspicion can be partly explained by numerous reports of Securitate loyalists emerging from manhole covers and from secret spots inside the subway and firing indiscriminately at civilians during the fighting of December 21-23. Several newspapers even carried reports of spectral terrorists emerging from false tombstones in graveyards around the city. How much of this can be substantiated is not clear. For nearly fifty years, the truth in Romania has been a state secret. It appears no less elusive now.

But Octave assures me the woman is wrong. "She's crazy. Don't listen to her. The Securitate left the tunnels over a month ago when they were told it was safe to come out. They're up here again. On the street. Just like before. Only the faces at the top have changed. Don't be fooled."

Later Octave accompanies me back to University Square. We pass the Athénée Palace Hotel, its exterior pocked with small arms fire. The tattered whore of Bucharest remains open for business, however, and we go inside for coffee. Seventy years ago, she was the playpen for the idle rich as well as a nexus for foreign agents discreetly buying and selling secrets. She didn't fare as well under the Communists, but during the 1980s the Palace had resumed a bit of her scandalous past, becoming the playground of rich foreign students from predominantly Arab countries such as Libya, Iraq, Syria, and Jordan. A center for black market money operations and prostitution, it was, like all hotels frequented by foreigners, also a major listening post for the Securitate. As in the gaudier InterContinental, all who worked here reportedly were agents of the police, including the prostitutes; the phones, rooms, restaurant tables, and bar were all bugged. The prostitutes working this hotel did so with official blessing, provided they reported everything they heard from their presumably grateful clients.

Here in the Athénée with Octave, I sip espresso in the nearly deserted bar. We've quickly developed an easy rapport, he and I. Exactly why I cannot say.

"You would not believe what went on in this place," he says. "Everywhere you looked, there were *curva*, all of them working for the Securitate. All of them spreading their legs for the Arabs." He shakes his head. "You have no idea what it was like."

Actually I do have an idea, thanks to my first night in Bucharest eighteen months earlier. I had fallen asleep just after my late arrival at the Dunărea, a one-star hotel (slightly above a flophouse on the hotel food chain) just across from the main railroad station. I awoke around nine o'clock, extremely hungry, but few restaurants were open at that hour. The hotel receptionist suggested my best bet would be the Hotel InterContinental, a twenty-minute walk across the city center.

The traffic had vanished along with the daylight. Fog settled over the city, and I hugged the sides of buildings during the walk across a mostly deserted downtown to the InterContinental, flagship of the ailing Romanian tourist industry. The rococo modern lobby would make a perfect set for an early Star Trek episode: tall, ribbed glass columns rose to a faintly illuminated, glitter-covered ceiling thirty feet above the tiled lobby floor.

The restaurant was nearly deserted. At the only occupied table, three Chinese in Mao outfits conversed in Romanian with a jowly, gray-faced man in a boxy pale-yellow suit. I felt I was in some almost cartoonish parallel universe.

The menu was extensive. I had not eaten in more than twelve hours and my stomach was protesting. I finally settled on "Chicken Paprikash—a Transylvanian delicacy."

The waiter, a short, stocky man with longish, slicked-back black hair and sleepy eyes shook his head. "I'm sorry, but we are out of that tonight."

"Well…what about the roast chicken leg?"

"We have no chicken at all. I'm sorry."

"A steak?"

He shrugged apologetically.

"The Transylvanian sausage platter?"

Again the shrug.

"What is this menu for, then?" I asked, genuinely perplexed.

"This menu," hissed the waiter very quietly as he leaned towards me, "is a work of fiction." Then in a louder voice, he said, "May I recommend the pork schnitzel, mixed salad (tomato, cucumber, and feta cheese, and fried potatoes?"

After the dinner, which was excellent, as was the bottle of Romanian Pinot Noir, I made my way to the bar at the top of what was allegedly the finest hotel in the city: "All the ameenities (sic) of a world-classic hotel at your finger tops," read the brochure I picked up at the reception desk on my way in. The Astro Bar featured a U-shaped bar around which were arrayed, in the latest 1970s style, orange Naugahyde stools.

On that night, a dim blue overhead light cast a sickly glow on three bored-looking women with too much makeup and very tight dresses. Two of them were bottle blondes, while the middle one sported a shade of red I have seen only once before: on Bozo the Clown. All wore black fishnet stockings. I was, apparently, a fresh prospect, and one of the women asked me where I was from.

"The United States," I said.

"Ooh, such lovely passports," she replied, switching to English. She smirked lewdly as the other two began to giggle. The bartender flashed them an irritated look.

"I am Corina," the redhead announced. "So, what room do you stay in tonight? Perhaps later we could have a party." She lowered her eyes in what I supposed was intended to be a demurely provocative look.

"I hope you mean the Communist party," I said, my head already swimming from the wine at supper.

This cracked all three of them up. Even the bartender.

"I'm sorry," I continued, "but I could never afford a room here. I'm staying at the Dunărea."

Corina's heavily glossed lips twitched slightly. "The Dunărea? God, what a dump," she snorted, her interest vanishing as suddenly as her smile. "Anyway, foreigners are not supposed to be in places like that."

As I tell Octave this story of my first visit to the InterContinental, he nods emphatically. "Of course she would say that. The Dunăera doesn't have microphones hidden in lamps; foreigners don't stay in hotels like that," he says.

"Why not? It was cheap and relatively clean."

Octave just looks at me for a long moment and shakes his head.

Our conversation returns to the tunnels. I wonder if they are urban myths, like the alligators living in the sewers of New York City. "Look," he says, "I am employed by the department of public works, and I have heard a lot of stories about these tunnels." He points to the floor. "Under here, they run. They run from the Presidential Palace all the way to the Casa Poporului."

"So, have you seen them?" I ask. "Or have you seen blueprints or maps or anything *definite*?"

He wags a finger. "No. Anyone who has seen them is now dead. I have never seen them. Thank God."

"Then how do you know they exist?" These tunnels fascinate me, and I really want to know.

Octave barks out a shrill laugh. "They exist. They exist because that is how Ceauşescu's doctors got him from the palace to the brand new clinic in the basement of the Poporului...for the transfusions."

I put down my coffee. "What transfusions?" I ask very slowly.

"Oh, everybody knows about those," Octave replies dismissively. "Every month they took him to this clinic where he received blood from babies."

"You mean like Dracula?" I am trying hard to understand where this conversation is going.

"Not like Dracula! This is no joke," he replies, his voice growing louder. Two men at the bar turn and stare at us, and Octave lowers his voice. "I don't think the babies died; they just took a little blood to invigorate him. Not all their blood. They come from the orphanages, you know. My mother knows about this. Everybody knows about this. Believe me."

I can almost believe him. It is true that transfusions are routinely given in Romania for a variety of ailments, but this is different. Still, it doesn't seem that incongruous, considering Ceauşescu's excesses and the country's mythic past. Anything in this place could be true.

Octave tilts his head toward the men at the bar, both of whom sport black leather jackets. "Rats," he says. "Securitate. As I told you, there's no need to hide in the tunnels. It's quite safe for them up here again."

Events less than two weeks earlier have left many like Octave bitterly skeptical of both the "revolution" and the new government's intentions.

On January 23, the National Salvation Front voted to run candidates in the May elections, despite a promise when the provisional government was formed that the Front would stay out of politics. Provisional President Ion Iliescu, the obvious Front candidate for president, defended the position, insisting that the decision was made only after a number of groups of Romanian workers had urged the Front to reconsider and become actively involved in the electoral process.

Three days later, on Sunday, January 28, the main opposition parties convened a huge anti-government rally protesting both the Front's decision to run in the elections and the presence of so many Communists in the provisional government. Demonstrators shouting "Down with Communism" called for its dissolution.

The next day pro-Front workers and coal miners stormed into the city, viciously beating demonstrators in the square where hundreds had died only weeks earlier. The miners then ransacked the three main opposition political parties' headquarters, sending hundreds to hospitals, many with fractured skulls and broken arms and ribs.

Following predictable international outrage, the Front agreed to open the governing council to opposition parties, satisfying one of the main contentious issues and temporarily quieting demands from those left out of the provisional government.

The men at the bar stand up and walk towards the door, and as they pass our table they flash us a hard, sour look. "They're all over the place. Still," Octave murmurs.

Alone now in the bar, he grows furious as he talks of the miners. He leans forward, clenching and unclenching his fists. "The government has refused to condemn those attacks, which many of us believe they were behind. We don't believe the invasion of those criminal bastards was a spontaneous show of support for Iliescu. Who do you think could get those special trains to transport them from the Jiu Valley to Bucharest? No trains from there ever ran on that schedule."

Now, two weeks later, relative calm appears to have settled over the capital, but Octave tells me that the next day—Sunday—demonstrators will again take to the streets, this time to demand the government surrender control of Romanian Television. "We will stay there all week if necessary," he says.

I ask how he can just take time off from work, and he shrugs. "No one is seriously working right now," he says. "What's the point? We don't even know who we're working for, and besides, no one's been paid in weeks. Anyway, this is more important. If we're not very careful, things will just return to the way they were."

While the airwaves clearly remain under government control, the face of the Romanian press has undeniably changed in the past six weeks. Today I have seen long lines at bookstores and newspaper kiosks, which have sprouted on every street corner as people finally have access to the outside world. It is a startling difference.

During my last visit, the musty offerings at most bookstores consisted mostly of the collected works of Nicolae and Elena Ceauşescu, as well as the works of Lenin and Marx. Now, the bookstores cannot keep up with the demand for Western writers and long-banned Romanian ones. Most surprising, however, is the proliferation of newspapers. At one newsstand I count twelve different publications. Prior to December 21, the dominant paper was *Scînteia,* the official publication of the Romanian Communist Party. Among the new ones now are *Adevărul,* the pro-Front paper; *România Libereă,* an anti-Front paper allied loosely with the opposition parties; and a number of lesser ones overtly aligned with the fringe parties.

But RTV, Romanian Television, the major source of news for the majority of the country, is far from free, and the issue of who will ultimately control the airwaves has become increasingly contentious for opponents of the provisional government, who claim that Iliescu has simply co-opted the former tyrant's monopoly.

Octave suggests we meet in front the InterContinental Hotel the next morning at nine o'clock for the march to the television station. "I predict at least ten thousand people will be here. This is a very important demonstration, and I think you will find this interesting," he says.

Here in this anxious, fraught city, everything is interesting to me, especially the dizzying contrast between Ceaușescu's sepulchral Bucharest and the near anarchy that has now engulfed it. Nobody seems to understand what is really happening. Octave, like many others, I suppose, regards this unfolding political drama with equal measures of confusion, hope, and dread.

"You need to be very careful," he continues. "You cannot know who is who."

I tell him I am fine alone, but he shakes his head and says that he has decided to be my protector. "No, you don't understand. You need a little watching, believe me. You will talk with anyone."

And with that, the matter is settled. I don't really know why he has taken this interest in me, beyond the obvious fact that we seem to have hit it off—and that he was impressed by my having been to Bucharest when Ceaușescu was still in power. "Americans never came here," he said. "Nobody came here. Why would anyone? Why did you?"

*　　*　　*

By a quarter to nine on Sunday morning, about six hundred people have assembled in front of the InterContinental. It remains cold, but now the sky has turned brilliantly blue. I look around, but there is no sign of Octave. I wonder about the possibility of violence, given the miners' visit two weeks ago, but even stronger is my amazement at the variety of people who arrive: old ladies in babushkas, old men with canes, factory workers, men in business suits, students, even children. Police presence is light, and what tanks I see have their turrets pointed skyward, their crews outside joking with a group of children cocooned in snowsuits.

The mood is festive as we begin the roughly three-mile walk from the center of Bucharest to the television station. People brandish handmade anti-government signs: "The TV is a stage!" "Wake Up, Romania, Don't Sleep!" "Democracy, Not Lies!"

"Nice day for a revolution," shouts a young man behind me as we pass a tank. The tank crew, who are leaning against the turret, nod and laugh. A bearded man wearing a beret holds a sign depicting the television station grasped by the tentacles of a huge red octopus. Another sign features a television with its top pried off. Out of it pours a fountain of iconic hammers and sickles.

"Join us!" shout the marchers, and bystanders along the route begin to filter into the growing line. People living in apartments flanking the route watch the progression from their windows, some clad in pajamas and robes with their breakfast coffee in their hands. Most wave happily at the constantly growing crowd.

At each intersection, hundreds of new marchers join the procession, and the chants get louder. But where is Octave? I keep expecting him to tap me on the shoulder, yet there is still no sign of him. I am not particularly concerned, however; I have plenty of film and tape, and if something were to go wrong, at least I would be in good company.

About halfway to the television station, the marchers pause. It is a touching moment as several thousand people kneel in silence by a simple but beautifully carved wooden cross festooned with red carnations and peonies. On it is carved "Glory and Peace to those who have died for freedom on December 21-22, 1989."

For a couple of minutes there is only the sound of engines, car horns, and the wind. Resuming the march, the column files into Victory Square in front of the old Foreign Ministry building, now the headquarters of the provisional government. Cordons of troops ring the building, but here, too, the long guns of the tanks point straight up, away from the crowd. The soldiers appear relaxed and, like the conscript in front of the Presidential Palace, very young. Some of the marchers hand soldiers peonies and chant *"Armata e cu noi"* (The army is with us). Others begin to chant *"Jos Comunismul!"* (Down with Communism!)

I hear the throb of engines, and a cloud of diesel exhaust wafts over the crowd as five more tanks roar by and take up positions in the square. Their sudden arrival is a little disconcerting, and within minutes we move away from Victory Square, away from the tanks that have now formed a tight circle around the government headquarters. Apparently they intend to take no chances.

As we approach the television station, evidence of the recent fighting is once again visible. Romanian TV is situated in a quiet residential district for the party elites, but now many of the houses across from the television building are gutted shells, their facades blown away by bullets. I am told that Securitate units took up positions in these houses to rain automatic weapons fire upon the television station in an attempt to drive out the army forces that had come to defend it on December 21. Groups of demonstrators now stand on the balconies of these gutted buildings.

Directly across from the television station a man stands on a roof waving a large Romanian flag with the center bearing the hated Communist symbols cut out. Here, too, tanks and soldiers surround the television building, ostensibly to defend the station from rogue Securitate units possibly lurking beneath the city—but I wonder. Again the turrets are aimed away from the crowds and the soldiers mingle freely with the demonstrators.

Many thousands now surround the television station. The crowd begins to sing "Where, oh where is the truth?" Then, a chant begins to build: "Iliescu, come out and talk to us! Why are you hiding?"

A group closest to the entrance of the station begins to chant, "Iliescu, take off your mask!" One poster shows Iliescu removing a mask of his face to reveal Ceaușescu beneath it.

The crowd continues to jeer. Hoping to get a better vantage, I approach a tank, where an officer reaches down and helps me up to the turret, which is pointed up, away from the demonstrators. "Ah, democracy," he says with a curious smile. So much of what is happening here seems odd and disjointed to me. I don't understand why the soldiers appear to be so lax, so sure that everything is under control. I am also not sure whom the army serves at this point, declamations of "solidarity with the people" notwithstanding. Here we are, a mob really, demanding that the government surrender what may be its most effective weapon of control: the airwaves. Surely *someone's* finger must be close to the trigger.

And then I see Octave walking towards me with a smile and a wave. The crowd is now chanting a new refrain: "Another revolution might be a good idea." Many of the soldiers laugh at this new message.

An hour later, an RTV camera crew begins filming the demonstration, but after a few minutes, it stops shooting and returns to the building. A station functionary announces over a crude public address system that because it is Sunday there is not enough staff to keep filming. The crowd boos, and most here doubt the day's events will be shown on the evening news.

Suddenly a new chant builds through the crowd: "LU-POI! LU-POI! LU-POI!" A stocky, bald man in a suit, overcoat, and scarf climbs on top of a tank to building applause.

Somewhat of a folk hero following his dramatic television appearance in December, the now immensely popular Mihai Lupoi was appointed Minister of Tourism by the provisional government, but on February 8, he abruptly resigned. Within hours of the resignation, a dump truck with no license plates ran a traffic light and smashed into his car. News reports indicated first that he had been killed; other reports maintained he had sustained serious head injuries and was a vegetable.

Now here he is three days later, appearing for the first time atop an adjacent tank bantering with the crowd. "Well, here I am again at the television station," he jokes. "But this time I can't get in." After raucous hoots from the crowd, he continues. "Quite alive, as you can see."

Pointing behind him towards the station, he continues, his voice mocking, derisive: "Don't believe everything you see on the news. They told you I was in an accident, but it was a deliberate accident, I think. I must tell you that I am very worried about the future of democracy in this country." Lupoi then tells the throng he is going home.

I push through the crowd, assisted by Octave, and together we catch up with Lupoi just as he steps into his car. I tell him I am an American journalist and ask if he has time to talk. "Not here," he says, scanning the street. He suggests we meet that evening in the lobby of the Hotel Bucuresti. "No one will do anything there," he remarks before driving off.

Nothing is resolved at this demonstration at which no Romanian Television officials or government representatives have spoken. When I ask about this, Octave glances over at the RTV building. "What did you expect? Iliescu to come out and give away the station?" he asks in dismay.

*　　*　　*

In the lobby of the Hotel Bucuresti later that evening, Lupoi and I discuss his resignation. Octave is now not only my bodyguard but my official translator as well. The three of us are crammed into a small booth in the bar at the far end of the lobby. Lupoi and I drink brandy. Octave sips a Coke. Dressed in a brown suit and a red V-neck sweater, Lupoi looks more like a college professor than a recently resigned officer in the Romanian army. "So," he asks, giving me a level stare, "Who do you write for? The *New York Times*? *Newsweek*? *Pravda* maybe?" he asks with a chuckle.

I tell him the truth, that I write for a very small paper in Vermont but hope to freelance this material to a much wider audience. "Well, at least you're honest... and smart enough to talk to me," he says. "The day after I resigned, as you know, I was nearly killed by a mysterious brush with a dump truck." Lupoi erupts in his odd giggle. "It wasn't so mysterious, really, was it?"

I ask him why he had resigned so suddenly, a question that prompted a snort.

"Shortly after assuming my post as minister of tourism, I realized that the tourism ministry was still a major center of Securitate activity and that its personnel there had not been changed since the revolution. A high-ranking colonel in the Securitate was assigned to the ministry. I demanded that he resign and he refused. He told me, 'My boss tells me to stay.'"

Again a shrug and the sardonic laugh. "Clearly he is working for Iliescu and not for me. So it seems the Securitate now work for Iliescu. There is no place for these people in a free Romanian government."

"So nothing has really changed?" I ask.

Lupoi sighs and takes a sip of his brandy. "It's more complicated than your question suggests. Of course things have changed. On the surface anyway, so now these pigs will have to be more careful. Ceaușescu is dead after all, and thank God for it. But they still have powerful friends who will need their particular services. There will be no dramatic arrests, no trials, no accounting for what has happened under Ceaușescu. Nobody's hands are clean in this country."

Lupoi rakes the lobby with his eyes and shrugs. "I should tell you that I and my family have been receiving death threats on the telephone." He looks at me in mock puzzlement. "I wonder who could be making such calls."

Lupoi has emerged as an opponent of the Front with a vocal public following, at least in Bucharest. His facility for public speaking and his easy rapport with the crowd earlier that day prompts an obvious question: Would he run in the elections? He shakes his head.

"Maybe someday I will run for president, but not now. I don't have the experience. I am not even forty."

Lupoi scans the room again. Sweat beads on his forehead, which he wipes with a napkin. He taps the table lightly with his left hand. "But right now, my main concern is for the safety of my family, so I don't know what I will do next." And then he erupts in that odd, nervous chuckle: "I just hope it lasts longer than my most recent position."

Five young people now approach the table. A tall, pretty girl in tight jeans and a red-and-black striped sweater smiles at Lupoi. He smiles back. "Can I help you?" he asks.

She shifts her weight awkwardly and stammers. "Mr. Lupoi, we are university students and we just want to say we admire you and will support whatever you want to do. If you make a political party, let us help. There are many of us."

"Thank you," he says. "I appreciate that. I appreciate that very much."

These students are staring at this slight, bald, unprepossessing man as if he were a rock star. I am amazed. Octave watches this scene slack jawed. Apparently, he too is impressed.

After the university students leave, Lupoi checks his watch. "I'm sorry, but I must go," he says as he stands. Octave and I escort him to the curb outside the hotel, and as he climbs into a waiting Dacia, I wish him luck.

"I think I'll need quite a lot of it," he says as the car lurches away from the curb. "And so might you if you are here for any amount time."

REUNION

The train chugs through the industrial landscape on the outskirts of Bucharest. A complex of soot-blackened cinderblock buildings and storage sheds behind a high concrete wall belches black smoke into the lowering early afternoon sky. From the ROMTEX sign above the factory gate, I gather it is a textile plant. A huge Romanian tricolor flag with the center ripped out is draped over one section of the wall. A sign that used to read "Victory to the Communist Party of Romania" now reads "Down with the Communist Party of Romania." Fluorescent lights flicker through a row of grimy windows.

I am in a second-class compartment for the six-hour trip to Transylvania and the mountain town of Covasna, where I will see my friend Gabby Szigeti again. When I said goodbye to him on a train platform in Sibiu nearly a year-and-a-half ago, I promised I would return, presumably under better circumstances for him and Romania. Sitting across from me is a youngish couple, maybe in their late twenties. They are bundled up in ski parkas, scarves, and toques. There is no heat in this compartment and the dampness seeps into everything.

Outside in the corridor, an old man and his wife stare out the window smoking, a large canvas tote bag wedged between them. Soldiers peer from other windows in the corridor. My train car seems to be half full, a very different ride from my last trip on this train, which was in the late summer and a world away. Those same picturesque villages, stripped of late summer lushness, now appear squalid and mired in mud. Wooden carts pulled by horses struggle through the deep, half-frozen ruts in the dirt road paralleling the tracks. In a clearing, a group of men cut cordwood with cross-cut saws, their labored breath steaming in the brittle February air. Smoke curls listlessly from crumbling stone chimneys.

After about a half-hour, the heater begins to emit faint but encouraging clanking noises. The woman reaches down and touches the cold metal, shakes her head, and sighs deeply. "Be patient," the man says. "The car will be warm enough next summer." They both laugh.

The woman extracts a large square of yellow cake from her rucksack. She breaks it into pieces and holds one out to me, smiling. This is one reason why I love the Romanians. Steeped in privation, they are nevertheless—or maybe because of this—very generous, especially to strangers on trains, it seems. I am riding one for the fourth time in this country, and for the fourth time, I am offered food or drink.

"*Poftim*," she says.

Poftim. It is a beautiful word. Like its Italian counterpart *prego,* it can mean any number of things, all of them gracious. It can mean a simple *beg your pardon?* or *please,* or *thank-you,* or *come this way,* or *after you.* The word is softer than prego, however, and is spoken like a kiss. From a woman's lips it is almost erotic; from a man's, it is gallant. I take the cake and thank her. "*Mulțumesc foarte mult,*" I say.

"Ah, you are Italian?" she says.

"No, American," I answer.

"And you speak Romanian?"

"A little," I say.

They ask if I am from New York, and I tell them no; I am from Vermont, a place they have never heard of. It is a very small state, I say, with farms and forests and mountains—not unlike the country we are passing through.

Then comes the inevitable question: Why do I know some Romanian? Before my first trip to Romania, I picked up a Teach Yourself language course, *Romanian: A Complete Course for Beginners*, an excellent investment. With a comprehensive grammar book containing numerous exercises and two audio cassettes, I plunged into a language that turned out to be full of surprises. I was immediately struck by Romanian's similarity to other Romance languages, especially Italian, and discovered it is the closest modern language to classical Latin. This fact itself struck me as fascinating—the notion of a Latin culture marooned in Eastern Europe and existing for two thousand years surrounded by hostile Slavs and Magyars was both improbable and compelling.

I reply to my cake-sharing friends with what has become my inevitable answer, one that has so far proven to be both true and diplomatic: "Because it is a beautiful language." My linguistic limitations, however, become evident after a few basic pleasantries, and the woman, who introduces herself as Celina, asks if I speak French. "*Oui*," I reply. Her husband is Stefan. Both are pharmacists in Predeal. We now continue in French.

Meanwhile, from my duffel bag I have extracted a loaf of black bread, some sausage, and a liter of wine, all of which join the cakes. Between the three of us, we now have a meal.

"So, what do you think of our revolution?" asks Stefan as he tears off a piece of bread. His stringy black hair bunches up around the upturned collar of his parka, which frames a sallow, chiseled face. He is very thin.

I tell him the only thing I can: "Too soon to tell, don't you think?"

Stefan shrugs. "I don't know. All of these demonstrations are interesting and at least they are not gunning people down in the streets, and that's an improvement."

"That's right," says Celina. "Now I can say what I want!"

"So what?" snaps Stefan. "I mean, what does it matter? What does it matter if no one listens?"

I ask them if they support the provisional government. Both are ambivalent. It is unquestionably better than what preceded it, but, they say, the country is in some suspended state. "There are always meetings and always pronouncements afterwards," says Celina, "but the television and radio are still controlled by the Front, so what can we know? Just look on the television, that's all you see—people speaking out. After all these years of holding so much inside, maybe we just don't know how to react to this new freedom."

Stefan nods in agreement. "I don't think we trust it. If you told me two months ago that such things would happen, I would not have believed it. Can you imagine?"

Events *have* moved incredibly quickly. Watching the formation of some kind of oppositional political landscape after almost forty years of tight, monolithic control is fascinating and dramatic. Unlike the Poles, Romanians do not have the advantage of an incipient government in exile; there was no Solidarity here. Nor is there the kind of comparatively liberal tradition found across the border in Hungary with its steady evolution towards democracy.

"What is going to be so hard for us is to be able to trust," says Celina. "Some people say Iliescu and the Front are all Communists, but so what? Everyone was a Communist. My parents were party members. *We* were party members. We all had to be if we wanted a job. It means nothing. The problem is that for so long we had this kind of paranoia. And now we wonder who among us were the informers. Maybe they still are." She sighs dramatically. "I'm tired of politics and we have just started." Snow begins to fall as the train chugs its way out of the plains and into the mountains.

There is still no heat, but the wine and conversation compensate considerably. At a small station, we stop. Out on the platform, ten or twenty Roma kids throw rocks at the side of the car, presumably to get our attention. Their faces are covered with dirt and in some cases with what appear to be scabs. Layers of ragged sweaters cover them, along with grease-stained patched trousers and shoes wrapped in layers of filthy cloth. The girls are in long tattered skirts.

One little girl, who looks about six, lurches up to the side of the car, her pleading eyes boring into mine. Her right leg below the knee seems to be attached backwards, as if some surgeon made a terrible mistake. Her foot points behind her at the base of a grossly bowed shinbone. It is a horrible deformity, unnatural and frightening in a way I cannot articulate. I drop a wad of Romanian lei out the window to her as the train jerks to life with a hiss and resumes the long climb into Transylvania. Without looking at me, she scoops up the money and retreats into the shadows, dragging her leg behind her. She leaves an erratic trail in the snow that has begun to cover the cement-tiled platform.

"You shouldn't have done that," Stefan says sharply. "You can be sure the parents are hiding just out of sight, there in the shadows by the building."

"So what? Why does that matter? These are children. I don't understand."

"They are *ţigan*," Celina says, spitting out the pejorative word like a bitter seed. "That girl you feel so sorry for? Well, I am sure her parents did that to her when she was an infant: they twisted that leg, little by little so people would take pity on her. A deformed child can do much better begging. Until a few weeks ago, you would not see this so much. The police would deal with them."

"This is horrible and sad," I say.

"Yes, it is. Both of those things, but they are Gypsies."

We lapse into silence, watching the snow fall on the deep stands of hemlock that hug the ravine. I am feeling cramped and go out into the corridor, where I light up a Carpati. The rough, rich smoke is soothing. Celina and Stefan's attitude about the child upsets me, but I will not press the issue. We are, after all, strangers, and I am from somewhere else.

Looking out the corridor window, I am dazzled by a wild landscape. The high cliffs of the southern Carpathians shimmer in the afternoon light, plunging almost vertically to the valley floor. Moving slowly, the train passes through villages that have remained largely unchanged since the Middle Ages: I wonder how much it really matters out here what or who the government is. This all feels so removed from Ceauşescu, from the turmoil in Bucharest, from the epic transformations beginning beyond this country's borders, and even from the twentieth century itself.

The land exudes something primeval. The Carpathian forests are deep and vast, home to bear, wild boar, and wolves. Rarely does one associate conservation with Communism, but in a strange twist, the worst intentions have led to unexpected blessings. Ceauşescu had decreed that only he and his appointed guests could hunt bear in these mountains. As a result, it is estimated that more than 60 percent of Europe's brown bear population now resides within the mountains of Romania. It is also a haven for wolves, and by 1986 the United Nations estimated nearly 40 percent of all remaining wolves west of the Urals live here as well. It seems fitting; after all, the wolves of Transylvania have been traced to legends as far back as the time of the Roman colonization.

This is a land of legends, many of them dripping with blood, some more famous than others. Transylvania is where the Pied Piper reputedly absconded with the town of Hamelin's children. Here too is the realm of Dracula, both historic and mythic. Watching a hawk lazily circle a stand of huge hemlocks, their almost-black boughs laden with snow, I think of Octave's assertions of Ceauşescu's transfusions from infants and of the strange Romanian proclivity for blood-drenched icons. Some assert that Bram Stoker's blood-sucking rendering of the historical Count Dracula was inspired by another Transylvanian, Elizabeth Báthory, sometimes referred to as the Blood Countess. She was preternaturally beautiful, with jet-black hair, alabaster skin, and eyes of curious luminosity. She was also, according to surviving legal documents from the Hapsburg Court, a hypersexual maniac with a taste for both witchcraft and monstrous sadism. As her beauty began to fade, she became convinced, partly through the instruction of her dwarf *majordomo*, that bathing in the blood of young virgins could preserve her youth indefinitely, and dozens of girls from the villages surrounding the castle began to disappear. In some cases, bodies were discovered drained of all blood. Eventually rumors reached the Hapsburgs, and the Hungarian king, Mathias II, sent a military expedition to her castle in 1609.

What the expedition discovered set down in court documents was monumentally horrific: the remains of 650 girls and young women were found in the network of passageways running beneath the castle. Elaborate chambers of torture had been set up as well, and everywhere was the residue of blood: spattered, pooled, and spilled. They also found cages of starving females awaiting rape, mutilation, and sacrifice. Many of these girls claimed to have been forced to eat the roasted flesh of others who had died before them.

In her subsequent trial, Báthory denied nothing, claiming that her status as a noblewoman gave her the divine right that justified anything she had done. Because of her family's connections, she was not put to death but confined to her castle for the last six years of her life.

How easy it would have been for illiterate peasants to attribute the loss of their children, the screams that periodically emanated from Báthory's fortress, and the grisly discoveries of bloodless corpses to something other than human agency. Cruel, indifferent, or monstrous governance has been a fact of life in this region since recorded time. Ceauşescu was perhaps simply a successor in a long dynasty of grief.

*　　*　　*

The daylight is fading fast now, and when I return to my compartment, Celina and Stefan smile at me. Perhaps they are uneasy with my obvious discomfort. I want to change the channel, shift the mood. "I want very much to hear some Romanian jokes," I say.

The request is not frivolous. I have noticed here a delicious mordancy, an ability to laugh at appalling circumstances. It is the universal humor of oppression. In a country where jokes were for so long the only practical form of oppositional behavior, humor assumes an almost magical power and poignancy. It is one of the best windows into a society I can imagine, and here in this freezing train compartment with the snow falling outside, I want to peer through that glass. For the next thirty minutes, I am practically assaulted with jokes, most of them very funny, at least to my twisted sensibilities:

"Gorbachev, Reagan, and Ceauşescu are at a meeting," Celina begins, leaning towards me. "The Russian and American presidents are bragging about their telecommunications industries.

They challenge each other to a contest. Reagan says the Americans could build a telephone line straight to hell and talk directly to the devil if they wanted. Gorbachev says the Soviets could do the same thing but much more cheaply. What about you, they ask Ceaușescu. He says he can do it cheaper than either of them. Because he is Romanian, of course."

Stefan interrupts: "Faster, too," he says.

"Yes, faster and cheaper," counters Celina. "So, a month later the three presidents meet. Reagan says the telephone line is complete and he has made a call to hell. He presents a telephone bill to prove it: Gorbachev and Ceaușescu look at the bill: 'That's expensive,' says Gorbachev, a hundred thousand dollars for three minutes!'

"'No problem for us,' Reagan says. 'All Americans are rich. And what about you, Mikhail?'

"Gorbachev pulls a piece of paper out of his pocket and puts it on the table. 'As you see,' he says, 'we too have completed the installation and made a call, but much more cheaply than your capitalist system!' Sure enough, it is only five-thousand dollars for three minutes.

"Then Ceaușescu laughs. 'Well, I have something to show you both,' he says. Reagan and Gorbachev are surprised. The president of Romania, the great Genius of the Carpathians, takes out a piece of paper and puts it on the table. It is a bill from Romtelecom. Gorbachev looks at the bill. 'That's impossible!' he shouts. 'This is some kind of Romanian trick! Three minutes, no charge. What kind of fools do you think we are?'

"Our great leader simply smiles. 'There is no trick,' Ceaușescu says. 'It's a local call.'" Celina starts to laugh.

She rummages through her bag and extracts three small apples. We bite into them, the snaps audible above the clack of the rails.

It is amazing to me how directly these stories reflect the vagaries and anxieties of life under the rule of a profoundly mercurial megalomaniac. One of the great Romanian pastimes under Ceaușescu was standing in line, and that is reflected in dozens of stories. People stood in line for sugar, salt, bread, eggs, cooking oil, and clothing. Stefan offers this one: "As anywhere in Bucharest, a line has formed and winds around the corner of a building. With each passing minute, another person joins the line. One man walks up and asks the person at the end of the line what he is waiting for. He doesn't know. So he asks the woman in front of him. She doesn't know, so she asks the person in front of her. He doesn't know. And so the question is passed all the way to the person at the front. He says he just stopped to tie his shoes and when he was finished, a line had formed behind him. 'Then why didn't you just walk away from this, if that is the case?' asks the man behind him.

"The man at the front responds: 'Are you crazy? And lose my place at the head of the line?'"

The wine is nearly finished now as the last of the daylight fades. The fluorescent light in the ceiling flickers a few times and goes on. It casts a feeble, pinkish glow over the small compartment. Celina clears her throat. "Here's one about our glorious legal system— well, not anymore, I hope. Two men are working at hard labor in a copper mine up north. One says to the other, 'What did you do to get fifteen years hard labor?'

"The other man shrugs. 'Nothing,' he says. 'I am innocent.'

"The first man shakes his head: 'You're lying. Nobody gets fifteen years for nothing. The normal sentence for that is ten.'"

Other jokes follow in rapid succession. A man goes into the post office and complains: "These new Ceauşescu stamps don't stick properly." The postal clerk leans over the counter and says, "That, comrade, is because you are spitting on the wrong side."

Celina and Stefan alternate, each trying to outdo the other. Clearly they have done this before. Faced with ever-worsening living conditions as Ceauşescu tightened down the screws during growing unrest and deepening economic crisis, Romanians reacted predictably: joke escalation.

The train is slowing to a stop as we pull into Predeal, where my traveling companions will leave. "Would either of you have told me these jokes two years ago?" I ask. Stefan's eyes widen. "You mean on this train?"

"Yes," I say, "on this train." Celina and Stefan look at each other and shake their heads. "Never!" says Stefan. "We never knew who could be listening."

*　　*　　*

I am alone in the compartment now, and the temperature seems to drop even more. Ice is forming on the inside of the window. I think of the letter my friend Gabby sent me a few weeks ago, a joyous letter full of hope. It was the first time I heard from him in eighteen months, since that night in Sibiu toward the end of my stay in the Socialist Republic of Romania.

I had been in Braşov for three days and was feeling restless. I wanted to rent a car and just wander into the mountains until I ran out of road. There was one car rental agency in Braşov—at the tourist office in the Capitol Hotel, where a lovely, dark-haired young woman stood behind the tourist desk counter in the empty lobby. Her nametag read Irina Cipianu, and she frowned slightly when I explained I wanted to rent a car for two days.

"Ah, then you will want a driver, of course," she told me.

"Well, no," I said. "I want to explore on my own."

She stiffened and her eyebrows lowered. "But where do you want to go?" she asked. "You could get lost."

"It really doesn't matter."

"I don't understand."

"It doesn't matter if I get lost."

She was now somewhere between exasperated and confused. "Does not matter?"

"I am on vacation," I explained. "I have no place to be at any certain time. And anyway, you can provide a map with the car, yes?"

She hesitated, then shook her head. "Sorry, but we are out of maps, for the moment." Pointing to a low-resolution map behind the counter, she continued, "We have only small copies of this."

"It must be a widespread shortage," I said. "In Bucharest, I couldn't find a map anywhere. Everyone told me the same thing. Out of stock. Maybe next month."

Irina Cipianu merely shrugged. "Such things happen sometimes, anywhere. It is normal."

I was amazed by her bland acceptance of what is "normal." However, a "temporary shortage" of maps was to be expected in a place where you could be jailed for photographing bridges or train stations. I gave her my best innocent-as-the-driven-snow smile.

"We must have some indication of where you intend to go," she insisted. "This is for your safety entirely."

I pointed to the mountains just south and west of Sibiu, another of Romania's ancient Saxon cities.

She brightened. "Ah, you want to see the resort at Păltiniş."

I nodded. I was completely unaware of this place.

"It is very beautiful," she said. "And all around are very authentic villages. Wonderful places, but mostly you will see nothing but mountains and sheep grazing."

"It sounds perfect."

She frowned, two tiny vertical lines appearing just above the bridge of her aquiline nose. "But there is no place to stay except in Păltiniş. I can make a reservation for you at this resort."

I said I would probably spend the night in Sibiu, which is only sixty miles from Braşov anyway. She seemed somewhat reassured by this statement. At least they would have some idea of where to look for the car.

Our dance continued. "So, do you have a car available for two days?"

"I will have to check. Please give me your passport."

She looked carefully at my picture, then back at me: The Socialist Republic of Romania was the only visa stamp in my passport.

"Mr. Shaw," she asked, exhaling softly. "What are you doing in Romania?"

"I am a tourist, trying to explore a little of your fascinating country," I responded.

"Please sit down," she said gravely, gesturing towards the couch across the cavernous lobby. "I will make some calls."

Five calls and one hour later, she beckoned me to the desk. She beamed. I smiled back. "Well, I have arranged for you to have a car." She said this with a clear note of triumph, as though she had achieved the impossible. For all I know, she had, but the sign on the desk *did* suggest this was a car rental agency.

"Now you must fill out a little paperwork and then you will collect your car."

The "little paperwork" consisted of three forms in triplicate, each requiring three official stamps, their significance I could not imagine. Irina drew a map denoting the major route numbers, making sure I understood the road to Sibiu was 1A, a main east-west artery.

Within minutes of leaving Braşov, I passed the edges of the new industrial part of the city. I saw no old neighborhoods, no tree-shaded narrow streets, just straight rows of depressingly identical apartment buildings sprouting from muddy ground.

Soon the industrial sprawl gave way to a road lined with Lombardy poplars, the bottom four feet of their trunks painted white. Traffic thinned to some tractors belching thick, black smoke, a few heavy trucks doing likewise, and an assortment of horse-drawn carts. I was traveling along a broad, flat plain, the road bisecting vast potato fields. It was harvest time, and several things surprised me: the hundreds of people stooped over digging potatoes and the lack of machinery. Horse and donkey-drawn carts collected the piles of dug potatoes, much as these people's ancestors must have done centuries ago. I thought of the official propaganda pictures of the rows of tractors chugging in unison across some huge, flat expanse bathed in sunshine, the triumphant marriage of agrarian socialism and technology. That marriage appeared to have soured, and I had read that overuse of huge machinery had greatly reduced soil quality, compacting once light, fertile ground into something more like cement. I had also read that shortages of fuel and fertilizer had further degraded food production, leaving quota after quota unfilled.

Although it was raining heavily, work did not stop. Near the road, two young women struggled to pull a burlap sack toward a central pile of potatoes. They were dressed in heavy, mud-spattered sweaters over long, faded cotton dresses. They were also completely soaked. Just beyond them was a road sign. Painted against a white background was the national logo, beneath which read the following in red letters: "Long Live Our Free and Independent Homeland, The Romanian Socialist Republic." I wondered how those women felt about their free and independent homeland and that ill-fated marriage.

I encountered a checkpoint a few miles beyond the inspirational signs where two police flagged me down to a stop. "Identification papers," one said brusquely. I handed him my passport. He looked at it closely, then at me. "Where are you going?" he asked, his voice a peremptory growl. I told him Sibiu. He nodded and pointed to the glove box. He barked out the words like bullets: "Let me see your registration." I opened the glove compartment door to retrieve the registration and the rental agreement. Finally satisfied, he handed them back and waved me on.

A few minutes later, the clouds cleared enough for me to see the mountains looming up just to my south, and I decided to leave the main road in the town of Săliște. One thin trail of horse dung followed the edge of the road, which almost immediately narrowed to one lane before starting to wind up into the mountains. The first few villages reflected the architectural heritage of the Hapsburgs, with even the small buildings bearing the traces of bygone grandeur: elaborately carved cornices and door and window moldings. Many of the buildings were painted in faded hues of gold, green, and blue. There was no roadside litter, excepting the lines of horse and sheep dung.

The Dacia's 1200cc engine was grossly underpowered, and it felt the climb. The car settled into second gear, a steady twenty-mile-per-hour chug. The road ascended through heavily wooded ravines, interspersed with steep pastures fanning upward from the valley. I passed through the small village of Rod, the mud-brick and plaster houses crowding up to the road's edge. Occasionally a four-wheel-drive ARO rattled past, but aside from that, I saw only a few men on horseback and the odd tractor. Periodically I passed little wooden shepherd huts far from the road, some with smoke drifting lazily from the chimneys and perfuming the damp air. The smell took me briefly back home to Vermont.

By the time a road sign told me I was entering the village of Tilişca, the air had grown cooler and was laced with a new smell—balsam. The road just ahead was temporarily blocked by several hundred sheep. I pulled up next to a dark-haired young man who watched them from about fifty feet away. He was clad in jeans, a white dress shirt, and a denim jacket—extremely fashionable attire in a place where jeans, American or otherwise, were at a premium. He put out his thumb in the universal sign, and I motioned for him to get in. High cheekbones and the faintest trace of a slant to the eyes lent a slight Mongol cast to a scrubbed, unlined face. He appeared to be in his early twenties.

"Thank you for stopping," he said. "Where are you going?"

I shrugged. "I don't know," I said.

He looked perplexed for a moment. "Are you lost?"

"No, I am in Tilişca," I said, pointing to the sign just behind him.

He laughed and climbed into the car, regarding me quizzically for a moment. "Do you speak English?" he asked.

"Yes."

"Good. Your Romanian is very—well, interesting," he said in perfectly accented, textbook-British English. "I think maybe you are from Yugoslavia."

I took some pride in at least having confused him, but clearly my two-month crash course in Romanian had not left me speaking exactly like a local. "No, America," I said.

He shook his head. "You are joking with me. Americans don't come here. Never."

"It's true," I said and showed him my passport.

"So where are you going?" he asked again.

"No place in particular, just driving around. This is all wonderful for me, all very interesting," I said as I pointed to the sheep, the terracotta-tiled roofs of the stucco buildings, and to the two shepherds leisurely following behind the flock of very healthy looking sheep. The men wore rough wool vests and conical hats. Each clutched a long, well-worn staff. "Where are *you* going?" I asked.

"Poiana Sibiului, to a wedding party. It's only a few towns away. It's a very nice place."

And so I met Gabby Szigeti—a fifth-year electrical engineering student at a polytechnic university in Braşov. He told me he was from the alpine village of Covasna, famous, he said, for its curative waters and several spas in the surrounding mountains. His parents, both elementary school teachers, lived just across the street from where they worked in a house that had been owned by his family for five generations. His grandfather, born under Austro-Hungarian rule, lived there too.

Beyond Tilişca, the road climbed to a plateau of undulating hills, mostly denuded of trees. Conical haystacks provided yellow counterpoints to the timeless, rolling green landscape. We passed lines of slow moving carts drawn by horses, some healthy looking, others emaciated. Men, women, and children rode inside them, along with pigs, chickens, potatoes, beets, and sacks of what Gabby told me was wool. "They're on the way to market," he said, explaining that the government allowed farmers to sell produce from their small private plots.

Because it was market day, the main square of Poina Sibiului was clogged with vendors selling garlic, onions, cabbages, beets, turnips, and tomatoes in stalls set up around the edges. At a rough wooden table in one corner of the square, a young woman in a red, black, and gold headscarf sold cakes and lime-flavored soda water by the glass. Other stalls offered odd assortments of nails, nuts, bolts, screws, clock springs, used Dacia carburetor parts, tractor coils, some old sweaters, work shirts, and rain coats; assorted trowels, screw drivers, pliers, and saws; fans in various stages of dismemberment; sheet music, accordions, and some beautifully crafted leather halters.

Our destination was a few streets over from the square—a quiet, shaded dirt road. We parked in front of a new, blue and teal house, a rambling one-story structure built around a central courtyard and set in a grove of birch and aspen just above a hillside apple orchard.

I felt a little awkward about crashing this wedding, but Gabby was insistent, assuring me that it was the third day of the party, and everyone was now welcome.

The front door led directly into the courtyard, at the center of which was a makeshift grill over a large bed of wood coals. About a hundred people milled around, glasses in hand, laughing loudly. The smells of wood smoke, roasting lamb, and garlic filled the air. A burly man with an unruly shock of curly gray hair squatted by the coals, turning the chunks of lamb. A blue apron protected his suit from the spitting grease. Seeing Gabby and me, he smiled, stood, and grabbed a bottle and three glasses. It was Mircea, the father of the groom (a university friend of Gabby's) and the host. He placed a glass of *ţuică*, clear plum brandy, in my hand, motioning for me to drink. I drank, of course—the 140-proof liquid burning its way to my stomach. Then, pulling me by the arm, he led me over to the fire pit. "Now, please, eat!" The lamb was exquisite, as were the tomatoes and feta, fresh bread, and homemade wine. I was also introduced to *mămăligă*, Romania's national comfort food. It is cornbread, baked over the coals, and then stuffed with melted goat cheese.

At the end of a short receiving line, Dorian and Maria, the bride and groom, bantered with friends and neighbors. They laughed easily, exchanging flirtatious glances as the line filed by. They looked to me almost too young to be married—more like a high school prom king and queen. Sitting against the wall in the central courtyard, I was struck by the warmth and buoyancy of all of the people in attendance.

Later, behind the house, I joined Gabby and his college room-mates—Zoli, Mihai, and Tsu. They were with Mircea's youngest children, who were playing a simple game: just beneath the house was an old shed with a chimney, the top of which stood about twenty feet away from us. They had collected a pile of wormy drops from the orchard and were trying to lob the apples into the small opening. Completely drunk, Gabby's roommates lost this game while the kids continued to lob apple after apple into the small opening. I had less luck but managed to land a few before Gabby signaled that it was time to leave.

By five o'clock, I was driving back down toward Saliste with Gabby, Zoli, Mihai, and Tsu. The Dacia groaned under the added weight, but fortunately we were then headed down from the mountains. The sky had cleared completely, and shafts of pur-ple-pink light bathed the plains below in an eerie glow. I offered to take them to Sibiu, where they planned to get an evening train back to Braşov. The price, I told them, was that they had to answer my questions.

"So, you *are* a CIA spy then?" asked Tsu, who was the drunkest.

"No," I replied. "And if I were, would I tell you?" This prompted more laughter.

During our ride down from the mountains I learned the following: All four were in their final year at university, a period they all agreed was "a lot of bullshit," which apparently meant they were doing unpaid internships at local factories apprenticing to staff engineers who, they swore, knew less than they. Their education, including room and board and tuition, had been paid entirely by the state, in return for which they must work for three years at a factory of the government's choosing, housed in grubby worker hostels. After that, Gabby said, they could work anywhere, provided there was an opening. It seemed a reasonable tradeoff, especially when compared to the cost of a college education for most Americans.

I asked them why there was no move towards revolution or change, especially considering the changes beginning to sweep through the Soviet Union and the rest of Eastern Europe. Gabby snorted. "I think maybe we are more lazy. Why bother? I mean, we have a biological solution. Ceauşescu and all of them are old men. Why bother to kill them when they will be gone soon enough? And then this will all fall apart. Nobody wants Communism."

"Enough politics," says Zoli. "It's time for a good Romanian joke. The regional party boss visits a village to inspect the sheep. He is out in a field and when he thinks no one is looking, he takes one of them behind a shed and starts to have sex with it. Of course the village mayor is watching, and he starts laughing. Do you know why?"

I shook my head.

"Because he picked the ugly one."

The last of the daylight was fading as we hit another roadblock. "You must say the right thing," Gabby told me. "Now you must say, 'Bună seara, domnule ofiţer; suge-mi pula te rog,' which means, 'Good evening officer, what is the matter?'"

I nodded. Tsu, Zoli, and Mihai attempted to stifle their laughter in the back, but they needn't to have bothered because I already knew what this meant: "Good evening, officer; please suck my dick." Of course, I didn't tell Gabby that as I rolled down the window. "Bună seara, domnule ofiţer," I said as Gabby jammed an elbow into my side.

It was a simple identification check; at least it started out that way. After I handed him my passport, the cop took the identification cards from my four passengers. I could follow most of what he said. Moving around to the other side of the car, he shouted at my passengers. "Where are you coming from? Where are you going? Why are you traveling with this foreigner?"

As the cop asked these questions, he recorded their names in his notebook, for what purpose I did not know. Gabby explained that they were hitching back from Poiana Sibiului and I picked them up on the main road. Of course they had no idea I was a foreigner when they got in the car. Eventually, the cop returned the identification cards and my passport.

"Are you guys in trouble?" I asked as we pulled away. I had no way of knowing the significance of an event like that one. There was no problem, I was told. "Just cops being assholes," Gabby said, but his laugh was uneasy.

"But can you get in trouble for being with a foreigner?" I asked. I recognized the word *străin* because it was in the fourth lesson of my Romanian course: *I am a foreigner: sunt un străin.*

"No, it isn't a problem, but if you were to stay in my family's house in Covasna, that would be trouble. Very big trouble."

Tsu suddenly began to gag. "Stop the car," Zoli shouted. "Tsu is about to make a political speech!"

I braked to halt by the side of the road. The rear door flew open, and Tsu lurched into a field where he began to retch loudly. During Tsu's "oration," Gabby and I discussed options for the evening. Was it possible, I asked, for them to join me for supper and then take a later train to Brașov? It was only seven, and Gabby was sure a late train would work fine.

Ten minutes later, Tsu staggered back to the car to loud applause, and we continued our descent from the mountains toward the restaurant Gabby recommended in the Hotel Boulevard.

The Boulevard was a large, hulking pre-World War I edifice in the middle of Sibiu, just off from the medieval center. It was long past dark when we walked into the dining room, a cavernous space broken up by several sets of fluted columns rising to the ceiling. Tsu remained in the car, curled up on the back seat.

As with other restaurants, The Boulevard's menu was imaginatively expansive, but to no one's surprise, we soon sat in front of plates of pork schnitzel, tepid fried potatoes, and tomato and cucumber salad.

Our conversation was in both Romanian and English, which attracted the attention of the occupants at the other three tables, especially four men in leather jackets halfway across the room. We were laughing about the trip to Sibiu in the car, about the Dacia's groaning springs, about the checkpoint, Tsu's "speech," and the unlikely confluence of events that brought us together. "I can't believe it," said Gabby. "Here I am in the middle of Translyvania, having dinner with an American. My parents will be amazed."

Zoli nodded emphatically. "Us too," he added with a crooked grin.

As we ate, the four men kept staring at us. "*Securiste*," muttered Gabby.

"*Curva* (whores)," said Zoli in a low whisper.

One of the men stood and began to walk towards our table. "And look, there's the ugly one," said Mihai, who had been mostly silent since we left the wedding party. This set the three of them off, and they erupted in guffaws. The man was then standing by the table, glaring down at Gabby. "Do you have a problem with us?" he asked in Romanian. I could smell his breath. We were not the only ones who had been drinking.

Gabby put down his fork nonchalantly, but I felt his right foot begin to twitch under the table. "I have no problem," he said. "We are just eating."

"And laughing," the man said with a nasty look, his eyes narrowing. "At us. Not a good idea."

"No, sir," Gabby answered immediately. "It is a misunderstanding. We have just been telling jokes, nothing mo-"

"Your papers. Show them to me. All of you." The order was loud and angry.

Apparently there was no question about the man's right to demand this.

Gabby fished out his identity card, his hand shaking slightly as he surrendered it. Zoli and Mihai did the same. When I handed the man my passport, a look of surprise flashed briefly across his face.

"Just a minute," he said to me in English before turning away and returning to his table with our documents.

We sat there in silence, humiliated by the intrusion, but even more than that, I was afraid for the three students who shared my table. "Don't worry," Gabby said. "They are just giving us a hard time."

I hoped he was right.

A few minutes later the man returned and handed back my passport and the other papers. His eyes riveted to my dinner companions, he said, "You should all be in school studying, not getting drunk with a foreigner in a hotel miles from home. You are returning to Brașov when?"

In response to what is obviously an order, Gabby told him they were taking the train at eleven o'clock. The man nodded. "Good idea." As he walked away, he glanced briefly in my direction. "Enjoy your stay in Romania, Mr. Shaw," he said, the faintest trace of a smile playing across his face.

It was damp and cold on the train platform. Tsu, Mihai, and Zoli sat on a hard bench smoking, talking softly among themselves. Gabby and I paced back and forth to keep warm while a jack-booted soldier leaned against the wall, periodically scanning the platform. At that moment, the mythical Iron Curtain was no longer an abstraction, and I felt bruised by what I had sought. What had been a joyous day was ending on a very sad and sour note for all of us. "Well, Zoli was right," I said. "He *was* the ugly one."

Gabby laughed, maybe just for my benefit. "It's nothing," he said finally. "Nothing will happen to us. He was just giving us a little fucking because he is Securitate. No problem."

"No problem," I repeated.

The loudspeaker announced the approach of the train to Brașov, which clattered into the station a few minutes later, its shrill whistle slicing the thick night air. A minute later, Gabby, Zoli, Tsu, and Mihai stood in the corridor outside their second-class compartment, their faces pressed against the soot-streaked window as the train pulled away. I waved until they were out of sight.

I felt very sad and stupid, there on the grubby train platform. I knew that I would be going home in a few days, back to the cozy mountains of Vermont. I knew I was an interloper and that my mere presence almost endangered some wonderful young people too naïve or reckless to take heed. For me, there was little risk. I could ask questions, pay the equivalent of six dollars for a meal and drinks for five at a hotel, rent a car, and wave my blue passport, knowing that I would soon fly home. But for those young people, their only hope seemed to be to wait for old men to die. And then what? The Securitate would still be there. And I feared they would cast long shadows over Covasna.

*   *   *

That bad night in Sibiu seems a long time ago as the train from Braşov to Covasna pulls into the tiny station. Time can be tricky: eighteen months by one measure, a lifetime by another, for so much has changed so quickly and so unexpectedly, or so it seems. I see a familiar, lone figure as I climb down from the train. It is Gabby, who grins broadly. "I can't believe you're here," he says, taking my arm. "*Everything* has changed, and you have come back to see it. This is wonderful!"

Gabby gestures towards a beige Dacia sedan, a much fancier version of the one I had rented. "Only the finest transport for you," he says. "This one, actually, is in very good condition as you will see when I turn the key. It runs like new."

All I can tell him is that I am happy to be here, as we sweep the snow off the windshield in a small town nestled in the mountains. I cannot explain more than that; how it seems a miracle to be invited into what appears to be a pivotal moment in Romania's history.

We bounce over deeply potholed roads through the darkened village center and then turn into a side street where we park across from a school next to Gabby's house. It is old, low-slung, set back about fifty feet from the road. In the shadows, an unfinished building looms up just to the left. A new hotel, Gabby tells me. Now nobody knows when or if it will be finished.

Gabby is right about everything changing almost overnight. This visit to his parents' house would have been impossible under the old regime, as foreigners were to be monitored at all times. The family would have been in big trouble for this simple act of hospitality.

A fit, slim man greets us at the door; it is Gabby's father, Sebastian. He looks like an older version of his son, the same thick hair, dark eyes, and lanky build. Just behind him stands his mother, Elena, also trim, also smiling.

We sit in the small living room in front of the TV, which sits on an elaborately carved pine table next to an equally ornate bookcase. Sebastian smiles at my obvious interest in them. "I made those," he tells me, "and all the rest of what you see," gesturing towards a few other carved bookcases. He pours me another glass of the local homemade version of Jägermeister: it is unspeakably foul, but I drink it nevertheless. "It's very good, isn't it?" he asks.

I nod. "I've never tasted anything like it," I say.

We have already eaten a delicious meal of *ciorba*, a distinctly Romanian sour soup, bread, cheese, sausage, garlic pickles, and wine. All of it was homemade, and all of it was wonderful. Now I am joining a ritual being played out across the country every night: the groping towards some political order—in plain sight it seems—right there on the television for all to see. Tonight a group from the newly formed Council of National Unity, consisting of opposition political leaders and members of the National Salvation Front, are arguing, as they seem to do every night, in this case trying to decide whether votes in a new parliament should be public or secret.

"Incredible," says Sebastian. "We are paralyzed in this country right now. And *they* are worried about this. The economy has collapsed. Most of the factories are idle, people are using the situation as an excuse to go on vacation. Nobody seems to be in charge of anything, and things get worse by the day. Thank God Ceaușescu is gone, but the bickering between all of these parties—more than thirty now—has to stop sometime. We need leadership, not anarchy."

Gabby's mother nods in agreement. Neither is sure about Iliescu, but they think he is better than any of the others who have stepped forward, at least in the short term.

"It is going to be a very complicated transition," says Sebastian. "Nobody knows what will happen now, but one thing is sure: at least we are free and that is the main thing."

By eleven o'clock I cannot keep my eyes open, and Gabby shows me to where I will sleep. "You will please have my room," he says. "I will sleep in the living room, no problem."

The room could belong to any kid anywhere. Photos line one wall: of a five- or six-year-old Gabby fishing with his dad; Gabby and what appears to be Zoli when they were about twelve, in toques and parkas standing beside a rope tow on a ski slope. A poster of the banned Romanian rock band Phoenix adorns one wall; a Beatles poster covers another. An East German *Prominent* transistor radio, a cassette player and a Soviet *Zenit* camera occupy the top shelf of a bookcase filled mostly with technical manuals on electrical engineering. The bed, like every bed I have slept in so far in Romania, is very firm, very comfortable. Outside the window, the snow falls slowly as I drift off, the sound of a barking dog echoing in the distance. Whatever the privations this family has faced under Ceaușescu, their lives were, in a material sense, secure. Gabby has his university education, his parents both have jobs across the street teaching in the elementary school. They have a snug house of their own and even a car. Although the mood outside of Bucharest seems to be calmer, I wonder what will happen to these previously well-ordered but circumscribed lives under a new and far-from-certain order. I am sure they wonder the same thing.

The next morning, we drive to Brașov, which lies only forty miles from Covasna. The sun is dazzling on this cold February day after a heavy snowfall. Zoli meets us outside of his grandmother's house on a quiet street in the center. He is very much as before, the same crooked smile, thick glasses, and easy laugh.

In the afternoon we will be going to Târgu Secuiesc, a small town where Gabby and Zoli have been working. They want to meet up with some friends for dinner. This morning, however, we will stay in Brașov. I want to walk around the center and see what had happened to this lovely medieval city during the fighting. "Fortunately, not much damage," Zoli tells me as we pass by the Hotel Parc's bullet-riddled façade. At the Andrei Mureșanu monument, an old woman in a brown overcoat and brown scarf lights votive candles on a makeshift altar. Wreaths of evergreens draped with the Romanian tricolor lean against the monument along with a crude wooden cross. "The Securitate shot down six people here one night," Zoli says. "I heard the shots from my grandmother's apartment. They were bringing supplies to the army troops who were fighting against the Securitate. They just shot them. Now every day people put flowers here."

In front of the Securitate headquarters another shrine is set up, this one for the victims who had suffered within those walls. Some of the ornate plasterwork is blown away, but mostly the building is as I remember it. "The municipal police tried to occupy this afterwards," Zoli says. "But they couldn't use it: people are just too angry now. I think there are too many ghosts maybe."

I can understand that feeling, having learned something of those ghosts and the Securitate's work in Braşov during my first visit to that city. That was on a fine, early autumn day on my second morning in Braşov, and I decided to take the tram to the top of Tâmpa Mountain, which looms above the old city. I set out across the old plaza and up a long series of steps to the tram entrance. As I waited by the loading platform, a clean-cut blond man in square sunglasses, blue jeans, and a leather jacket was showing a record album to the tram attendant. I was understandably surprised to see him holding a copy of *Hank Williams' Greatest Hits*, and I asked him where he had managed to find the record. Then came the inevitable reply: "Where are you from?"

Realizing I was American, he switched to English. "This is, I am sure, the only copy of this album here in Braşov. I came here today to get it," he said, clutching it to his chest. "From a private collector. You must know Nashville, yes? You've been there, of course."

I told him no, to his evident disappointment.

Paul was a medical technician from Deva, which is on the far western edge of Romania, and like many in this part of Transylvania, he was ethnic Hungarian. He told me this regime singled out Hungarians for especially harsh treatment. "It's not good here, now," he said. "When Ceauşescu dies, maybe things will get better. They have to. He is insane, the politburo are all senile."

Paul had a good job, but he was thinking about trying to flee across the border to Hungary. The new and comparatively liberal regime there had recently been offering political asylum to ethnic Hungarians, an unprecedented situation in the Eastern Bloc. So much for the "fraternity of socialist republics."

The tram took us to a clearing high above the city, which afforded a view of the entire region spreading out beneath us. "Something terrible and interesting happened here last year," Paul told me. "The winter before last, at the tractor factory, thousands of workers revolted and went on a rampage."

I looked at him surprised; no word of this had reached the Western media.

"No, it's absolutely true. The government passed a law that if the workers did not meet their quotas, they would have to work Sundays for free until the production figures were met. That was it. It was like a fuse Ceaușescu or those other bastards lit. Imagine, all those workers standing out front of a factory they had set fire to, ripping open their shirts and facing the army units that had been called in. 'Kill us!' they cried. 'Shoot us! We won't live this way any longer.'

"And then a strange thing happened. These soldiers, kids mostly, refused to shoot. Or to do anything. So, the officers ordered them back to their barracks and they called in the Securitate forces. They shot into the crowd and some people were killed and many more injured, and two hundred of the organizers were taken away. Nobody knows what happened to them."

"Somebody must know," I said.

Paul shrugged and looked gloomily out over the city, still clutching the Hank Williams album against his chest. "This is not a normal country. Nobody is doing anything."

"Why do you think that is?" I asked. "Look what's happening in the Soviet Union, in Hungary."

Paul shrugged again. "We don't have a Gorbachev here, and this isn't Hungary. This is Romania."

Later that afternoon, after I left Paul to his Hank Williams album and dreams of Hungary, I stopped at a souvenir stall that seemed to specialize in all things Dracula. Brașov has a special significance in the life of Vlad Tepeş—the historical Dracula—who periodically lived at a castle built by his grandfather in the nearby village of Bran. The castle was undergoing a thorough restoration, the government hoping to establish it as a major tourist attraction.

It was from here, legend has it, that Dracula launched his most notorious massacre, the impaling of thirty thousand merchants and boyars in Braşov in 1459. Ancient woodcuts show a forest of the dead and dying impaled on stakes set in concentric rings, with the count feasting at a table in the center. On that day, the blood reportedly flowed so heavily it ran down the streets of the upper town. One priest apparently had the temerity to complain about the stench of blood and excrement coming from this mass execution. Ever obliging, the count had him impaled on a stake high above the rest so he would not have to experience the smells.

Staring at me in the souvenir shop were rows of mugs, cups, and plates, all bearing the iconic likeness of Vlad: lean face, high cheekbones, piercing, dark eyes, full beard, and hawk-like nose. I found it disquieting that a man of such violent proclivities should be universally respected by his countrymen, most of whom, at least on first impression, seemed to be almost disturbingly passive. What kind of people, I wondered, would have such a monster as a national hero yet continue to submit to Ceauşescu's vagaries? Perhaps the answer was in the question itself.

As I pawed through a rack of tacky faux-peasant blouses, I noticed a man staring at me. It was a neutral look, neither hostile nor friendly, but intent nevertheless. He immediately turned away when I returned his gaze. Was I being tailed? Surely the Securitate had better things to do on a warm fall afternoon.

Leaving the stall, I headed towards the main square, and to my dismay, the man followed me discreetly from a distance. As we approached the square, however, he closed the gap and walked up behind me. "You an *American*, son?" he asked softly in an accent that was pure Dixie.

Damn. I did not want to encounter another American on this trip to the dark side of Europe. I wanted no Cokes, no McDonalds, and certainly no fellow countrymen. Still, I nodded at the man, who now stood next to me. Wearing a plaid red, brown, and yellow short-sleeve shirt, corduroy slacks, and nondescript brown leather shoes, he was not dressed to call attention to himself; he could have been from anywhere in Europe, East or West. He appeared to be in his fifties with close-cropped gray hair, dark eyes, a long, thin nose, and a mouth like a paper cut.

"What gave me away?" I asked.

He simply pointed to my boots. His voice was raspy, granular, gravel in a tin can. "What in *heaven's* name are you doing here?" he asked.

"Checking things out," I replied.

"Are you crazy? This is no place for an *American,* not if you want to stay out of trouble."

He stood back and regarded me with both disapproval and concern before extending a hand. "Name's Whitaker. Grady E. Whitaker, US military retired."

We shook hands. It was now clear there was no way I could avoid him.

"Well, then," I asked, "What are *you* doing here?"

He looked around the street before responding. "Checking things out." He smiled thinly. "Just like you."

"And your impressions?"

Whitaker shook his head. "*That* is for another time. But if you want to hear an interesting story, I'll provide one, and supper. Be my guest—I'm at the Capitol. Eighteen hundred hours?"

"Sure, thanks," I said.

I was increasingly curious about Grady E. Whitaker, US military retired. I began to think CIA, and thoughts of James Bond frothed to the surface. Perhaps this encounter wouldn't be so bad after all.

Grady Whitaker stood outside the four-star hotel as I arrived at precisely six o'clock. The evening was warm and soft. We shook hands. He checked his watch.

"Right on time. That's good. That's very good," he said. "Glad you could make it."

The Capitol was an ugly glass and concrete building sitting just across from a small park bordered with stone benches and bisected by rows of yellow and orange marigolds and red salvia. The hotel was cold, graceless, and entirely functional, all right angles, concrete, and windows, somebody's idea of elegance in the late 1960s. It was also, no doubt, expensive. On the way to the dining room, we passed the tourist office, and I smiled at the woman behind the counter.

"Don't get carried away," Whitaker said. "They're all government agents here in this hotel."

"You mean that lovely lady behind the counter?"

Whitaker sighed. "That lovely lady behind the counter knows your passport number, your age, where you are staying, and probably what you had for lunch."

The huge dining room was nearly empty. Ten waiters stood by, leaning against the far wall talking quietly among themselves. This was, I supposed, another example of how to achieve full employment. "They serve an *excellent* schnitzel here," Whitaker said as a grave young man in the usual Romanian maitre d' attire—red vest, white shirt, black pants, black tie—escorted us to a table. As soon as we were seated, he deposited two menus on the table with a flourish. I knew enough by now to appreciate the sadistic irony of this gesture.

Whitaker asked him in heavily accented Romanian to remove the flowers from the table.

The maitre d' frowned. "Remove the flowers?"

"Yes, please."

"You don't like the flowers?"

"I am allergic to them."

Again the frown. "But they are plastic flowers, sir."

"Yes, exactly." Whitaker smiled broadly. "I am allergic to plastic flowers. Remove them now, please."

The man shrugged and with slow reluctance took the flowers away.

My host leaned towards me and talked *sotto voce*: "They often have bugs in them. You can't do that with real ones, the water's a problem. Let's keep the conversation general, you know?"

He looked at me intently, making sure that I did, in fact, know. I was beginning to suspect that the man across from me was a paranoid wacko, but at the same time I wanted to believe otherwise.

I was also hungry, and I put these thoughts aside long enough to study the menu. I began with the fish dishes: smoked lake sturgeon, pickled carp, fresh trout grilled with lemon and garlic, steamed prawns, whitefish in tomatoes and olives. I counted eighteen pork dishes including stews, cutlets, grilled chops, and stuffed medallions. Several steaks were offered in addition to about a dozen chicken dishes. I found eight varieties of salads besides the usual.

"Don't bother with any of that," Whitaker said.

"I know," I replied. "Just thought I'd see what I'm not getting."

Whitaker was right about the schnitzel; it was excellent, as was the wine. Between bites, he told me he retired from the army in 1983. "I'd been stationed in Frankfurt for many years, went native, and married a German woman in '76."

"What did you do in the army?" I asked.

"I was a chaplain. Now I'm just a plain old pastor."

My face must have betrayed my surprise because Whitaker laughed—the first time I saw him do this. "It's true. This is what I do. From a solider of Uncle Sam for twenty years, thank you, to a soldier of God. He's a much better C.O., I'll tell you that."

"Do you think you'll go back stateside?"

"Maybe, but I have no family back there in Louisiana. All dead now. Only child. All my family is in Germany. My wife is one of nine, and we've got two of our own. Like I said, I've gone native. German is second nature now. Been speaking it for almost twenty years and I grew up around it. My grandfather came from over here. Guess it's just the circle looping around."

Whitaker pulled out a wallet, flipped it open and handed it to me. "That's Joanna, my wife."

I stared at a middle-aged, buxom, brown-haired woman with a ruddy complexion and a warm smile, a blond boy on either side of her. I found it a little disquieting that this total stranger would show me this picture. A spy certainly wouldn't do that. "They're lovely," I said and handed the wallet back to him.

He smiled broadly, nodding. "Yes, I am blessed. And what about you," he asked. "Wife? Kids?"

"No to either at this point," I replied.

He regarded me sadly for a moment. "Ah, well, I hope that comes to you. No greater comfort than the love of a good woman. One of God's greatest gifts."

I nodded. I did not think a conversation about enjoying the "love of a good woman" outside of matrimony would be fruitful at this point, and I changed the subject. "I couldn't help noticing that you speak a little Romanian. How'd you pick that up? We're not talking a universal language here." I also wanted to ask him what a plain old pastor was doing in Braşov, but his earlier suggestion about keeping the conversation general stopped me. I watched Whitaker's eyes rake the still-empty dining room.

"After supper we'll watch the men play chess," he said. "They take it very seriously."

Near the hotel, dozens of old men sat on benches that flanked the park. They hunched over chessboards, and although the daylight was almost gone, I pictured sea lions sunning on the rocks in Monterey Bay. We watched the men, studies in threadbare dignity with their mismatched old suit jackets and pants worn to a sheen, berets rakishly tilted on their heads. They were born into the twilight of the Austro-Hungarian Empire, propelled by World War I into the post-war interregnum of Hungarian citizenship, and then by World War II as borders and alliances shifted, assimilated into the Romanian state, where they now sat, plotting moves and countermoves in the waning light of this early fall evening. In the background, strains of accordion music seeped from a tinny transistor radio.

We left the park, crossed the street and continued walking. A little farther on, Whitaker pointed to a graceful, unassuming building. "Do you know what's inside?" he asked.

I shook my head. "I have no idea."

"Hell is inside. This unassuming gem is the Securitate headquarters. I have a friend—we'll call him Zoltan—who knows this place very well. Like me, he's a pastor. He had been holding prayer services in his home, which the authorities here say is against the law. Services can only be held in 'approved' churches. They brought him down here last year for their first conversation. They told him to stop or there would be serious consequences. That was all. A little conversation, a clear warning."

"But he didn't stop?"

"No. The home prayer meetings continued, so they brought him back for another conversation. This time, to make the point clearer, they cracked a few ribs, broke his jaw, and knocked out a couple of teeth. The third time, they beat his feet to a bloody pulp with electrical cable; he couldn't walk for two months, which they told him would give him plenty of time to reconsider. But he didn't reconsider, and the meetings resumed. Finally, they burned his house down, apparently unaware that his wife and child were inside. That was six months ago."

"Have you come here to visit him?" I ask.

"No. He's no longer here. We have moved him somewhere safe."

"We? Who?"

"People who can't ignore the pain and humiliation of millions of our brothers and sisters in Romania, and in other places too." Whitaker and I were now in the middle of the main square just in front of the Black Church, a fifteenth-century landmark built by the Saxons when they populated this part of Transylvania.

An ice cream vendor rattled past us with his pushcart, and we bought two cups of strawberry ice cream. Between bites, Whitaker continued. "As I said, I'm a pastor, but our congregation is dedicated to certain—how shall I put this—outreach activities."

"You're just an ole' country preacher, right?"

Whitaker chuckled, a form of mirth of which I had not thought him capable.

"What kind of outreach activities?" I asked.

He shrugged. "Smuggling Bibles, mostly," he said, taking the last bite of his ice cream.

"Bibles?" I looked at him blankly for a moment. Microfiche concealed in a tube of toothpaste, maps of military installations glued into the binding of books, or Warsaw Pact war plans I could see, but not this. "Why Bibles?"

"Because people are desperate for them. They are not sold. Here it's riskier than transporting heroin. Transport and sale of Bibles is illegal, highly illegal. Standard jail term is ten years hard time. That's where we come in."

"How do you do this? Isn't it very dangerous?"

Whitaker paused, choosing his words very carefully. His Louisiana drawl was more pronounced now. "There is risk involved, but we have our network and our methods, as well as sympathetic customs agents and border guards. My colleagues are very thorough and very clever. Beyond that, I won't say."

By now it was well past dark, the square nearly deserted. I was becoming increasingly nervous following these unexpected revelations. Whether they were true or not, I had no way of knowing, but I felt he was telling me the truth. And if that were true, I was both humbled by his courage and aware that being in this man's company could turn out to be a liability.

Whitaker was inexplicably nonchalant about the possibility of being arrested. "I'm not involved overtly in any way that is likely to implicate me," he said. "I'm here as a tourist. In my case, I'm researching old church graveyards and doing brass rubbings of selected tombstones."

The conversation turned briefly to less serious matters, specifically the upcoming pennant races and German beer. As we neared the hotel, Whitaker's voice lowered. "You need to be very careful, son. Believe me, I know what I'm talking about," he said. "Be careful who you talk to, and watch your back. Always watch your back."

As we began to walk back down Strada Republicii, two cops sauntered past, gave us a hard stare for a moment, and then walked on. A little farther down the darkened street, laughter and the frenetic violins of Gypsy music floated up from a beer cellar, in front of which a group of men argued loudly. One of them had a split lip and a black eye, his white shirt spotted with blood and ripped around the shoulder. Another leaned against the wall vomiting, his body convulsing.

We turned down a side street and a few minutes later Whitaker and I shook hands in front of the Capitol. "Good luck," I said. "What you are doing takes a lot of courage."

He shook his head. "Courage doesn't have much to do with it. What Zoltan did takes courage. Living here in faith takes courage. I'm just a delivery boy with a safe home on the other side."

Whitaker gazed across at the park. "It all looks peaceful enough here, but this country is going to blow and when it does, it won't be like what's happening around it," he said. "It will blow hard. When the fuse is lit, it's going to be here in Transylvania, dollars to donuts. Maybe here, maybe in Timişoara, or Arad, but it will come. And I think soon."

I watched him walk briskly through the glass doors, back straight, face forward, soldier of God. Alone, I crossed the street and returned to the Securitate headquarters, which in the dim light of one street lamp had assumed a more ominous cast. I wondered if anyone was in there right now being interrogated, and if so, for what? Was someone being tortured? I listened carefully for cries, for the clank of a cell door, for the muffled crack of gunfire. But I heard nothing. Behind me on this quiet and quaint corner, a trolley clattered by and Whitaker's raspy drawl echoed in my mind: "Watch your back."

*   *   *

Standing in front of the former Securitate headquarters again on this bright February day, flanked by Zoli and Gabby, I wonder what has become of Grady Whitaker. I wonder too about his friend Zoltan, for whom a return to this city might be impossibly painful. I take one more look at the flowers in front of this building and then we walk to the car.

Târgu Secuiesc lies just twelve miles northeast of Braşov, up a lightly traveled road between two low ridges. We pass a few horse-drawn carts, and a few trucks, but mostly we have the road to ourselves in the fading afternoon light. Our first stop is to see Gabby's "worker dorm" just outside the center of town. It is in a neighborhood of identical streets, flanked by identical apartment buildings: five stories, pre-cast sections apparently hastily thrown together. Paint and plaster peel from the sides, and huge cracks snake down exterior walls forming intricate spider webs around windows and expansion joints. "Yet another triumph of Romanian engineering," says Gabby. "These buildings are less than ten years old yet they are crumbling, as you can see."

Inside, things are not much better. Pieces of concrete are missing from the stairs, the railings working loose from the stair landings. The smells of garbage and backed up septic mingle with cabbage in the stairwell as we walk five flights to the top. "Our penthouse," Gabby says as he opens the door to a square room with three beds and a TV on a battered packing crate in one corner. The bottoms of the walls are painted a sickly green, the tops a dirty beige. Purplish gray linoleum covers the floor. "I only stay here during the week," Gabby explains. "Zoli only stays here if he's been drinking. That means both of us stay here during the week. No one is in the third bed right now, so we have it pretty good."

Zoli sniffs the rank air. "Anyway, it's very cheap and sometimes now there is even heat." He cranks open the window and carefully pulls on two ropes that are attached to a box hanging over the side of the building. Inside is an assortment of jars wrapped in a blanket: yogurt, jam, pickles, and a large bottle of Ciuc beer, a local favorite. "We are very civilized here," Zoli says gravely as he opens it against the corner of the window ledge. "Warm hearts, cold beer, and freedom!" he says and passes it to me.

"Not everybody has your luck," Gabby says. "You have seen the glories of the workers' paradise."

An hour later, we drive about ten minutes through the deserted old city center, illuminated only by the odd streetlight, and onto a side street, where we park in front of another anonymous apartment block. We are going to visit Gabby's friend Petyr, a computer programmer. Gabby locks the car and we start to walk away. I remember my Nikon, which along with an assortment of lenses is in a case on the floor. Gabby unlocks the car, I retrieve the case, and then he locks it again.

"You could have left it," Gabby tells me. "It would be safe there, believe me. This isn't New York, you know." He and Zoli laugh.

To our relief, Petyr's apartment is warm. He is a tall, stooped man, with long curly hair that is beginning to gray. His wife Anna is a plump blonde woman with outsized glasses, a beautiful smile, and a soft voice. Over dinner of cabbage, fried carp, potatoes, and pickled peppers, I ask Zoli to tell me more about the events in Braşov during the fighting.

"It was very strange. That's the only word for it," he says. "Things started later in Braşov, a day after Bucharest began to come apart. Here the army came into town and began passing out rifles to anyone over fifteen who wanted to help fight the Securitate. It's crazy, all these people running around with guns, none of them having any idea what they were doing. Many innocent people were killed this way, by idiots with guns who fired at anything that moved. A man down the street from me—I grew up with his kids—went on his roof to adjust his TV antenna and someone shot him. He fell off the roof and died. Not from the bullet but from the fall."

"How many people died in Braşov?" I ask.

"Nobody knows," Zoli says. "Officially it was a couple of hundred, but I think it was maybe a lot more. There was shooting all over the place. The Securitate would flag down ambulances and just open up the doors and fire into them, into the bodies of the wounded."

"This is true," says Petyr. "I know people who actually saw this."

"It was bad," Zoli adds. "Eventually, no one would drive the ambulances. Other things happened too. A lot of people in town would bring hot tea and bread to the soldiers on guard because they were cold and hungry and fighting for us. Some Securitate women infiltrated and brought tea with poison in it to the soldiers, and I heard a number of them died. After that, they would not let anyone near them."

I have heard stories about attempts by the Securitate to poison the water supply. I ask Zoli about this. "Oh yes, that is absolutely true," he says.

"But how do you know?" I ask. "Was someone caught with poison?"

"No, but everybody knows this," he says.

It is ten o'clock when we leave the apartment, and the snow has begun to fall again, this time heavily. Halfway down the block,

Gabby stops, staring at where the car should be. It is gone. He turns to me and laughs uneasily: "This is some kind of trick, isn't it? You have hidden the car!"

I wish that were true, but it isn't. And I tell him so. The car is gone, vanished, stolen.

"Oh my God," Gabby moans. The quaver in his voice tells me he is near tears. "This is a terrible thing for my parents. Oh my God!"

I find myself wishing again that someone has indeed played a joke. The loss of this car will be a terrible blow to Gabby's family. It took them many years to save money for what is a rarity among Romanians—a car—and replacing it will probably be out of the question, at least in the foreseeable future.

Back inside Petyr's apartment, we try phoning the police, but there is no answer. "Someone is there at the station, always," Petyr says. "The bastards just won't answer the phone."

After a few more tries, Gabby decides to walk to the police station, which is about two miles away. Zoli and I join him at a brisk walk through town in what is turning out to be a serious snowstorm. We see no cars, certainly no police, and no streetlights are on.

"Look around you," Gabby says. "You will not find police after dark because they are afraid to come out."

"Why?" I ask.

"Because people associate them with Ceauşescu and they hate them. Some have been very badly beaten just because they were cops. So now, they never travel alone, and never ever come onto the streets at night."

The police station is located in a dingy two-story building in a cul-de-sac. A couple of Dacias with *POLITIE* written on the side are parked by the building. Gabby pounds on the door. Through a window we see a reception area with a desk, and beyond that another room dimly lit by a lone light bulb hanging from the ceiling. "The bastard is in there asleep," Gabby says. Zoli and I walk around to the side of the building and peer into a widow. A man in a blue uniform lies on his back on a cot, mouth open, eyes closed.

"Bastard!" Zoli mutters and begins to pound on the window. Eventually the man sits up and stares out the window at Zoli and me screaming at him through the class.

"Go around to the front door," he shouts.

We rejoin Gabby at the entrance. The cop slides open a small window in the door. "What do you want?" he snarls, his voice thick with sleep. "It is the middle of the night." Alcohol fumes waft through the opening.

"My parents' car has been stolen," Gabby says. "We need help."

"Come back in the morning and file a report," he says. "There is nothing I can do tonight. Probably there is nothing I can do tomorrow, but come in and file a report. It is missing now, so don't worry. It will still be missing in the morning." He laughs sardonically.

"Why not now?" Gabby shouts. "It has only been a little while. I could give you the plate number and the registration! You could maybe radio the highway police or something."

"They are asleep too. Come back in the morning," the cop repeats and slides the little window closed.

We walk back through the snow to the "worker dorm," which takes us nearly an hour.

Mostly we are silent, and by the time we trudge up the steps, past the feral cats by the garbage, we are extremely cold and wet. This is going to be very hard on Gabby's parents, the loss of this car, and for once there are no jokes between him and Zoli, no wisecracks, no bravado.

Gabby sits with his head in his hands on the edge of his bed. "If only I hadn't borrowed their car," he groans. "None of this would have happened."

"You can't look at it like that," I tell him. "If I hadn't come to visit, then you wouldn't have borrowed the car in the first place. That makes it my fault, doesn't it?"

Zoli starts to giggle. We both look up at him in surprise. "If only I had been that man on the roof adjusting his TV antenna, I wouldn't have to listen to you two," he says.

The logic is beautifully Romanian, and we finally begin to laugh. I am almost asleep when Gabby speaks again. "It's not all bad, I guess. At least this has been a great night for sex for my family."

"How do you figure?" I ask.

From across the room in the dark, Gabby says, "Well, we all got fucked."

We take a bus back to Covasna the next morning, where Gabby tells his parents they no longer have a car.

"Perhaps they'll find it soon," Elena says without conviction, her mouth set in a grim line.

I feel partly responsible, but Sebastian quickly dismisses this. He assures me that they can find another car. "It's no one's fault but the thieves," he says, adding, "and maybe the police."

I spend much of this last day in Covasna with the Szigetis in front of their television as the political situation in the capital seems to be on the verge of unraveling. Newscasters on RTV offer contradictory accounts of threatened attacks against government ministers by unnamed forces linked to "foreign agent provocateurs." The government warns of dire consequences.

"This is bad," Sebastian says. "Very bad."

SOMETIMES EVEN PIGS GET TO PLAY

I return after five days in Transylvania to find Octave waiting for me in the lobby of the Union Hotel. He is with a very agitated couple, both of whom smoke and pace. The man draws deeply on a Carpaţi, exhaling furiously as he glares at the man behind the counter. The same nasty receptionist is on duty, and he is yelling at all three of them.

"Get out of here," he shouts. "This is a hotel, not a waiting room in a train station. You stand around here like hooligans and Gypsies. If you don't leave, I will call the police."

The man with Octave suddenly lunges to the counter and grabs the receptionist by the lapels, shouting into his face. "Maybe you should just shut up, mister. This is a new country now and shits like you have no place here! We've had enough of spies and fucking cops! We are free to speak with anyone we want."

Octave is horrified by the sudden violent turn and reaches out to restrain the man. "Are you crazy?" he shouts. "Stop it!"

Reluctantly the man releases the lapels, and the receptionist backs against the wall, his face flushed with rage. This seems the perfect time to ask for my room key, which I do with exaggerated politeness. I take the three of them to my room, away from the officious, nasty toad behind the counter.

Upstairs, Octave introduces me to Nadia and Codru, colleagues from work, who stand sullenly against the wall as Octave paces. "I don't know what is going on," he says. "There was a demonstration today at the Foreign Ministry building to protest the Front, and something has gone wrong. There have been provocateurs, and people have been hurt, maybe killed. At least that is what we are hearing on the radio now."

Octave tells me that earlier in the afternoon a crowd of anti-Front demonstrators had gathered at the Foreign Ministry building. He had been at the demonstration and says terrible things are now happening there.

Early in the afternoon the crowd removed the flag from the building. "Then," he said, "people started to enter the government headquarters. It was the strangest thing because there were soldiers there, and they did not try to stop anyone." Codru nodded emphatically. "He's telling the truth. Some of the soldiers actually helped people into the building. They joked and smiled. Nobody there wanted any trouble."

According to Octave, about a thousand people roamed through the building. "We were really more curious than anything else. But there were others, not part of our group at all. They were drunk, and loud, and seemed to have some kind of plan. They began to destroy offices, you know, smash furniture and break windows. I heard they attacked some people, but I didn't see anything like that. I just don't know. We three got out of there as soon as the trouble started, right before the paratroopers came. I think we were the last ones out before they surrounded the place. I don't know how many are still there or what has happened to them."

I suggest we go to the ad-hoc government press center that had been set up on the second floor of the Hotel Bucuresti just a few weeks earlier. Maybe there we can find out something. Nadia and Codru leave us outside the Union, and Octave and I walk the half-mile to the Bucuresti.

The streets are nearly deserted and the city seems calm with no indication of the trouble at Victory Square. This seems to re-assure Octave a little bit. By the time we arrive, the press office is closed, so we park ourselves in front of the television in the lobby. A Christopher Reeve movie, *Somewhere in Time,* is just ending.

Finally, RTV's version of events appears on the news. The broadcast shows thousands of people screaming "JOS ILIESCU (Down with Iliescu)." The camera then shifts to inside the building. A woman angrily holds up a book by Ceauşescu; the camera lingers on broken windows.

And then a bandaged Gelu Voican Voiculescu, the deputy prime minister, is interviewed. He tells the cameras that he was brutally attacked by drunken hooligans. "You can see plainly," he says, pointing to his ripped clothes. "They did this and they broke my nose." The announcer then solemnly reports that two soldiers have been badly beaten by the "frenzied mob."

These two soldiers appear on camera, sad eyes looking out over bandaged faces. One of the soldiers then corrects the announcer. "No one hit us," he says. "We were hit by flying glass when a window shattered."

I suggest we go to the Foreign Ministry building. "Are you sure you want to do this? It might not be such a good experience," Octave says.

"Well, it will be an experience of *some* kind," I tell him. He shrugs, and we leave the Bucuresti.

I have been acutely aware of the precariousness of the social and political situation here following the December events. While I regret not having arrived a month earlier, I feel lucky to be able to witness whatever is unfolding now, and I share Octave's concern that whatever happened and is happening at the Foreign Ministry could mean serious trouble, either for the fledgling government or its opponents. From Codru's and Octave's accounts, this could be the beginning of a set-up, some kind of Reichstag revisited.

Everything seems quiet as we walk the mile to the scene of the afternoon's excitement. The square in front of the Foreign Ministry building is still lit with arc lights, but now the inner perimeter is ringed with elite paratroopers, obvious in their blue berets. The outer ring remains manned by regular troops, who talk freely with the demonstrators, of which there appear to be about fifteen hundred.

There is an odd sense of disconnection here. Octave becomes distraught again when he learns that still no one knows how many people remain in the building or what has happened to them. A light snow has begun to fall, and it is getting colder as the wind picks up. Suddenly a window shatters on the second floor of the ministry. It is an ugly sound, and I sense a different mood among some of the people surrounding me. Scattered groups in the crowd, distinctly different from most of those still here—old men, professionals, women, and children—begin to hurl rocks at the building; some use flashlights to light the targets. Shouts of "bravo" punctuate the shattering of glass. More rocks are hurled, and more windows shatter. The rock throwers are all young, thuggish, and apparently drunk.

The soldiers close ranks and push us all quickly back to the perimeter by the road. "I told you this might not be such a good experience," Octave says nervously, and he may well be right. One of these soldiers tells Octave that two soldiers are dead—killed earlier by demonstrators. This totally contradicts what we have just seen in the lobby of the Bucuresti.

I tell the soldier that he is mistaken: the two wounded soldiers were on the news an hour earlier and did not appear to be seriously hurt. Once again I am struck by how young most of these troops are; they're nothing more than kids, totally unprepared for the duty they now face. Our conversation is cut short as an officer glares at this young conscript, who then reluctantly retreats into line.

A young woman in a bright-red overcoat tells me what I already suspected, that no one has been killed. "I was inside and I can tell you no soldiers were killed. The soldiers tell us that those who were in the building have been released, but no one here has seen anyone come out," she says. "I cannot understand this."

No sooner has she spoken when an old man with a Lenin-style goatee points to the building: "I heard a colonel say there are now thirty people still held inside the building."

A fat, middle-aged woman pushes her way forward and contradicts him, thrusting her face towards me. "Well, I know for certain there are four left."

Most of the people here seem to be demanding the release of those still inside the building, but no one has any idea how many, if any, are still being held. Someone else insists that three to four hundred are still imprisoned in the basement. For me, only two things are clear: nobody has any idea of what is really happening, and there are two distinct groups in this crowd. One of them is bent on trouble. The situation could get very weird very quickly, but I have to see how this will play out.

By eleven o'clock a new rumor has begun to circulate: those remaining (however many) have been injected with a sinister new drug.

"This could be true," Octave says, informing me that many Romanians fear surgery for a peculiar reason. "All anesthesiologists are secretly working for the Securitate and they are required to administer anesthesia in a specific way," he explains as we watch the soldiers watching us. There are more of them now.

"How do you know this?" I ask, fascinated by this impromptu lesson in pharmacology.

"I already told you. My mother is a pharmacist, so I know these things," he replies matter-of-factly, his eyes still fixed on the soldiers standing across from us. "The hospitals always order scopolamine along with the other stuff. It is similar to sodium pentothal, you know, and if you are having surgery, they first give you scopolamine. My mother says the really good anesthesiologists are able to prolong this stage of the anesthesia to extract as many confessions as possible."

Octave's lecture in anesthesiology is interrupted when the same group who had begun to break the windows suddenly begins to hurl rocks at the soldiers. "Rats!" they scream. Beside me a woman angrily shakes her fist at the rock throwers: "You are the rats," she says. "Go back into the sewers. This was a peaceful demonstration..You don't belong here. *You* are provocateurs!" Others nod in agreement.

The soldiers have again closed ranks, and this time they have taken the precaution of putting on their helmets. Next, they raise their AK-47s and point into the crowd. They now seem dazed and terrified, caught in the middle of something incomprehensible. I wonder if they will fire on us, and for the first time, I see the real possibility of something going horribly wrong. Octave worries too, but we decide to stay.

Then the bright lights in the square go out, and three additional tanks take their place in front of the building. Their turrets and guns, now pointed into the square, are *not* covered.

It is now well past midnight, and the arrival of the additional tanks, their motors growling in a low idle, have had their desired effect. They, along with the damp, cold night air, have tamped down a situation threatening to get out of control. The crowd has left, and only a few stragglers remain, huddled in small groups. The trouble boys are not among them.

On a very cold walk back to my hotel, Octave and I ponder the obvious questions: Who were the rock throwers? Those who ransacked the building? Those who beat up Voiculescu? Were they in fact provocateurs, and if so, for whom were they working? Iliescu? Or somebody else? Why did the soldiers help people into the building earlier in the day? Who made the decision to issue no orders? How many, if any, had been arrested? How many had been trapped in the building, and what was their fate?

Back in my hotel room with these questions running through my mind, I find sleep elusive. Worse still, I can't shake a horrible image of Ceaușescu receiving a transfusion from a baby.

*   *   *

The pounding at my door startles me awake. It is barely daylight, just past seven o'clock. "Tyrone!" a voice shouts from the hallway as I stagger out of bed and reach to open the door. Octave rushes into the room.

"Something is going on," he says gravely. "We have to go."

I want another two hours of sleep. "Something is *always* going on here, Octave," I mutter as I get dressed. "Go where?"

"Back to the Foreign Ministry. There are rumors Iliescu is going to speak tonight. And the miners are coming back."

This is not good news, at least about the miners. Downstairs in the small dining room we wolf down bread, greasy sausage and strong black tea. Octave hands me a copy of *Adevărul*, the government newspaper. Iliescu has scheduled a "special speech" tonight in front of the Foreign Ministry building at eight o'clock. He has urged "all those who support freedom" to come. There is no mention of the miners, but an inside editorial denounces the violence of the day before, branding the event an "assault on our legitimate government by fascists in the control of foreign interests."

More troops are visible this morning as we walk back to Victory Square. The mood is different, the tension palpable as grim-faced paratroopers surround the building while workers on cherry pickers begin the extensive repairs to the windows. People wearing NSF armbands hoist signs proclaiming ILIESCU DA! and JOS FASCISTI! signs in the plaza facing the soldiers.

A man dressed in work clothes and a patched black parka watches me for a few minutes as I photograph the shattered windows. Finally, he approaches. Through thick spectacles he looks at the damaged windows, then lights a Carpați. Once again I am hit by that uniquely Romanian potpourri of heavy Balkan tobacco, diesel fumes, coal smoke, garlic, and alcohol. His jaw is clenched, his mouth set in a hard line. "It's a farce," he says.

"What is?" I ask.

He spits and gestures toward the shattered windows of the Foreign Ministry. "All of this nonsense. These hooligans and fascists who oppose the Front. The miners are coming back today." He smiles grimly. "They will put a stop to this business. Their last visit was too brief."

Octave steps between us and barks at the man. "The miners are pigs. *They* are the fascists. *They* are the thugs!"

The man ignores Octave and looks at me intently. "Come back tonight and hear Iliescu. You might find it interesting." Then he turns to Octave. "Sometimes even pigs get to play, my friend," he says quietly before turning away. "Maybe they will play with *you.*"

The fact that Iliescu will speak tonight is significant. Even after the miners' last rampage and the demonstration at the television station, he has remained basically silent. And now, suddenly, it is announced he will speak tonight. The city is full of wild rumors: he will declare martial law, he will resign, he will launch a series of old-style raids on opposition parties and close down newspapers critical of the government. I have no intention of missing this speech.

By five o'clock that evening, trainloads of miners—thousands of them from the Jiu Valley—have appeared once again in Bucharest, thanks to a convoy of mysteriously commandeered trains that have brought them nearly three hundred miles across the country. And with them has come the specter of more violence. They are back with the same alcohol-fueled rage that propelled them through this city on their orgy of violence a few weeks before. Now they have circled the building, re-enforcing the phalanxes of nervous soldiers.

They are an odd sight in this place of odd sights, ghostly, menacing apparitions from a dangerous and dark underworld. Hard, gaunt faces are blackened with coal dust, as are their heavy blue-gray shirts and pants; clouds of cigarette smoke drift past the dim lights strapped to their dented blue helmets. The miners have not arrived empty-handed. They wield an assortment of clubs, chains, rubber truncheons, shovels, and heavy hammers.

In Romania, coal miners have long commanded respect for having endured the abject hell that is the Romanian coal mine and for having stood up to the Ceauşescu regime, securing for themselves significantly higher wages than other workers. And now they are feared as well. Their brutal assault on opposition parties and students two weeks ago has guaranteed that. Even as they gather here in Victory Square, their leaders are upstairs extracting yet more wage and work rule concessions from the provisional government—a devil's bargain for their loyalty.

By the time Iliescu appears, the crowd has grown restless. While most have come in support of him, pockets of Front opponents are visible, their signs equating Iliescu and the Front with Ceauşescu held aloft.

Octave and I walk around the square, which is now brightly lit. Romanian Television crews have taken up their own positions.

Finally, Iliescu's voice booms from loudspeakers spread strategically around the plaza. "Good evening," he begins, and a roar of approval explodes in the damp February night. "Thank you, my friends, for coming."

In measured tones, he begins his denunciation of the past two Sunday demonstrations as the work of counter-revolutionists. "I urge you all," he shouts, "all you supporters of democracy, to protect this new government from the dark forces of fascism—from those who would re-establish the old order."

A massive cheer erupts all around us. Raising a fifty-year-old ghost, Iliescu compares those who were involved in yesterday's disturbance to Antonescu's fascist Iron Guard. "Beware of the fascist *golani*," he tells the crowd. "Beware of spies among us."

"Listen to that Communist bastard!" Octave says. "Golani— that is exactly the same word Ceauşescu called anyone who disagreed with him. That's what he called the people who were killed in Timişoara and here. It's the same shit from a different asshole."

As Iliescu has been talking, the miners have begun to replace the soldiers guarding the Foreign Ministry building, leaving groups of elite troops to wander through the crowd. Octave is sure they are looking for people involved in yesterday's disturbances. Occasionally, someone is taken away—for what or to what I don't know. Octave eyes the soldiers but says nothing.

A sweet-faced, matronly woman standing next to me looks at my camera and microcassette recorder hanging from straps around my neck. "Tell the world," she says shaking her head angrily. Tears run down her face. "This is a nightmare, a big lie. Many people have been deceived. Yesterday was the product of provocateurs paid by the Securitate or the Front." She snorts bitterly. "There is no difference."

She touches my arm. "This is a circus. For weeks, no one from the government found a minute to talk to us. But now when the miners come, all of sudden here is Iliescu. This looks just like old times, like Ceauşescu times. The bad old days are back."

The television cameras are rolling. Unfurled Romanian flags minus their old Communist middles wave in unison with chants of IL-I-ES-CU! IL-I-ES-CU! This, no doubt, will be shown all over the country, unlike the demonstration at the television station the week before.

Thousands of miners now have massed here under the klieg lights. They shout at Iliescu: "Tell us what to do! Do you want us to stay tomorrow? Can we help?" Iliescu tells the miners that everything is under control.

"Thank you. Thank you, my friends," he intones. "Go back home and go back to work. We need you to do your jobs!" And then, he adds darkly, "But stand ready. Ready to return!"

The miners will not go home just yet, however. They have not traveled three hundred miles simply to show their support. They split up into small bands and begin to rove through the crowd, targeting obvious Front opponents, smashing their signs and knocking them to the street. Chains, clubs, and heavy boots find their marks easily.

Out of the lights and in the shadows, we watch four members of a Danish television crew begin filming one of these beatings, but immediately a group of miners surround the men. "Get out of here," they yell. "This is none of your business. Get out of here if you want to live."

An arching chain smashes a video camera from the hands of a tall, bearded blond man. Three uniformed police stand by, but they make no effort to intervene. They stand there, inert, impassive, perhaps even entertained by the unfolding drama. The mounting violence is appalling to me, senseless and horrific. To the police, however, the miners are obviously allies, but nothing nobler than hate and rage drive these thugs in their brutality. They are enjoying this little outing in the big city, and we can expect no help whatsoever from the police.

Sometimes even pigs get to play. Maybe they will play with you.

For the second time in two days I am frightened, but the fascination outweighs the fear. Of course we are not safe here—nor is anybody around us at the moment—yet I also want to see how this will all play out. Will the police or the army step in? I listen for gunfire, but there is none. Just the sounds of fists and sticks and chains smashing into flesh, just screams and curses. I stash the camera and cassette recorder.

Men in leather jackets have now appeared and accompany the soldiers who walk through this mess, looking intently at the faces of anti-Front demonstrators. Octave glances quickly at them. "Look at those bastards," he says under his breath, as he gestures towards the thuggish men with the flat, indifferent eyes of sharks. "They're still here, you can see for yourself. They don't even try to hide it. Please, we must get out of here. I was here yesterday, and they'll recognize me. We need to leave. *Now.*" Octave's voice is pleading, insistent.

The tall, bearded Dane has crumpled to the ground clutching his wrist as a couple of miners kick him viciously in the ribs. One of them glances over in our direction. I cannot see his face clearly but I feel the heat, the rage, and the menace implicit in the turning of his attention towards us. Octave is right: It is *definitely* time to go. We back away from the crowd and walk toward the relative sanctuary of darkness across the square.

About fifty yards away, three Leather Men grab a young man by the arms, and despite his protests, half push, half drag him to a waiting unmarked Dacia. His face is bleeding.

As we hide in the shadows—refugees from this mayhem—a white car slowly drives around the square. It stops almost in front of us, and a bald, bullet-headed man in a white trench coat climbs out. He stares balefully at what has now degenerated into a massacre. Octave and I recognize him immediately: Silviu Brucan, former dissident, former ambassador to the United States, and Iliescu's recently departed *éminence grise.* He became a political liability last week after insulting the country's emerging egalitarian sensibilities by hinting in a television interview that many people perhaps did not deserve to vote. "What kind of election, what kind of democracy will there be? We have in Romania twenty million stupid people and maybe two million smart people," he told a stunned nation. I saw him make that statement and marveled at his candor. Such honesty in my own country would be unthinkable. He has not appeared in public since then.

We continue walking away from the melee around the far side of the square, farther into the darkness. The fog has rolled in again, thick and nearly viscous. We find it comforting and begin to relax a little.

"I don't live far from here," Octave says. "Please, walk with me to my house. If I am with a foreigner, I don't think anyone will give me trouble now that we are away from the square."

It is the least I can do for my new friend, and as we walk, talking loudly in English for the benefit of hostile ears, Octave continues to curse the miners, the Securitate, and Iliescu. "They are all shits! There isn't going to be any democracy here. We have endured Ceaușescu for thirty years, for what? We just want to live in a normal country. Can you understand that?"

"Yes, of course," I respond. That is one of the few things I *do* understand after three weeks in "Free Romania."

We are now a few blocks north of Victory Square, where the streets are surprisingly quiet. This is a residential area, devoid of streetlights, and with the fog, visibility is nearly zero.

After about a half-mile, we stop at a waist-high iron gate, beyond which a dim light shines in a small window. I can see nothing else. Here we say our farewells, for I will be leaving for the US in the morning. Standing in the damp, cold fog, I am worried for Octave and for this country, but I don't need to tell him that. What fragile hopes he has had may already be dead, and along with them, the promise of a future free of fear. I don't know what to say, really, so all I do is thank him for all his help as guide, translator, and companion during these days. We hug. "Good luck," I say as he closes the gate behind him.

By the time I return to the Foreign Ministry building, it is nearly midnight, and I am relieved to see that most of the crowd has dispersed. Gone are the news crews, the miners having retreated behind the line of blue berets in front of the Foreign Ministry. They sit in clusters around makeshift fires, drinking and laughing loudly.

The ground is littered with broken placards, shreds of clothing, and occasional puddles of what I think is blood.

I begin walking towards the Union Hotel along Boulevard Balcescu. In the cold early morning hours, Bucharest again feels as it did during my last visit. But so much has changed so suddenly that it seems inconceivable that life could return to what it was when Ceaușescu ruled a cowed and compliant nation. What will replace it, however, seems as vague as the rumors that hover above this sad city.

The damp, nearly frozen fog stings my face. A battered Czech Škoda, its license plates conspicuously absent, draws up beside me and slows to a crawl. I think immediately of the plateless dump truck that slammed into Lupoi's car. The front passenger window rolls down as the driver switches on the dome light. Five men in leather jackets watch me walk. The man in the passenger seat is unmistakably one of those who had been circulating earlier at the demonstration, a thin man with long, stringy black hair and a pock-marked face. As if to give me a better look, he now turns his head towards me and draws his index finger across his throat. Maybe not so much has changed after all. I keep walking.

The Škoda keeps pace for about five minutes. Still looking straight ahead, I imagine being dragged into the car to suffer any number of unpleasant consequences. I am very close to panic, and my heart is doing drumrolls, the taste of fear metallic and sour in my mouth. It is only with great effort that I maintain this measured pace. I think of a little kid whistling past the graveyard, but in my case the ghosts are all too real and all too close. I begin to curse myself for having been so stupid as to leave peaceful Vermont in the dead of winter, however much I wanted to see this unfolding of history. Stupid, I tell myself. Stupid, stupid, stupid.

I think about ducking into a side street, but the main drag might be safer, deserted as it is. I glance to my right, and in a courtyard surrounded by a crumbling Deco apartment building, four dummies hang in effigy. Around each is a sign: ILIESCU/CEAUŞESCU.

Then the Škoda's windows roll up. The light switches off, and the car vanishes into the fog that has once again engulfed this strange city where two-legged rats scurry through tunnels beneath the streets bearing Kalashnikovs and serious grudges.

ACROSS THE RIVERS
Republic of Moldova, 1998

The tall, thin man behind the hotel reception desk leans forward as he puts down his cup of espresso, patting his lips primly with an oversized red linen napkin. He shakes his head slowly. "Terrible, just terrible the things we hear about over there." He tilts his head slightly to the left towards the frontier that lies a mere twelve miles east of Iaşi, once the Romanian capital and a city noted for its culture, universities, and lavish civic architecture. His Adam's apple bobs as he lowers his voice to a conspiratorial whisper: "In some of the villages, the old people are starving, sometimes they have to eat their own dogs. And in other places, young men are selling their kidneys for American dollars. It is a sad, sad mess over there. They are a basket case."

I find it interesting that Romanians, among the poorest of the former Eastern Bloc satellite nations, see themselves as lucky compared to the Moldovans, who are poorer still, poorer than the Serbians, Bosnians, even the Albanians. Some measure of contempt is also involved. Invariably the "stupid" jokes in Romania feature some hapless Moldovan rube, and many Romanians feel the Moldovans are slow moving, lazy, and dull-witted.

On the train from Cluj-Napoca to Iaşi, I heard a number of these Moldovan jokes. In a typical one, a little boy comes home from school with good news. "Papa!" he cries, "I was brilliant today!"

"And how were you brilliant today?" asks the father, a high government official.

"Instead of taking the bus, I ran behind it and saved us three lei!"

The father boxes the little boy's ears, and the child begins to cry.

"Why did you hit me?" the boy says through his tears.

"Because you are an idiot!" screams the father, his thunderous voice shaking the pictures on the wall. "You should have run behind a taxi. Then you would have saved us *twenty* lei!"

At the bus station, I purchase a ticket for the two-hour trip to Moldova's capital, Chişinău. The bus, however, does not arrive at its scheduled time of two o'clock. An hour later, Alex, a student from the university in Chişinău who has also been waiting with the rest of us by the bus gate, returns from the terminal with bad news. "The bus isn't coming," he says. "The motor caught fire in Călăraşi. It will be hours before they send another."

Alex points to a late-model black Opel parked across the street. "That man is going to Chişinău and has offered to take five people for the price of our bus tickets: you can get a refund in the station," he says.

"Do you know this person?" I ask.

"No, but I'm sure it's okay. This happens all the time."

Twenty minutes later a carload of strangers is heading toward the border. The Opel follows the road winding out of the hills of Iaşi down onto the undulant lowlands by the Prut River, which for more than one hundred miles forms the border with the former Moldavian Soviet Socialist Republic. My fellow passengers consist of two young girls, their lugubrious mother, Alex, and me. The driver, a dour, beefy man named Igor, collects our money with a wan smile. He sports what seems to be the fashion in this part of Europe, the Euro-thug look: very close buzz-cut hair, long sideburns, black jeans, polyester button-down shirt, and an oversized, garish watch.

At the Moldovan border, we are told to exit the car and go inside with our bags. I present my passport with the visa issued by the Republic of Moldova embassy in Washington.

"Purpose of your visit?" the crisply uniformed guard asks.

"To visit a friend."

He gives me a hard, sullen look: "Who is this friend and where will you be staying?"

Even during my first visit to Romania during Ceauşescu times, I had not been greeted with such peremptory rudeness, and I wonder if the arrogance of empire still clings, however absurdly, to what is now the poorest and among the smallest nations in Europe. I pull from my wallet an official Republic of Moldova Ministry of Interior business card. On it is Major Tudor Petrov's name and title: Head of the Legal Department. The man's demeanor suddenly changes. Smiling now, he points to the hard benches lining the wall of the border station. "Welcome to the Republic of Moldova, sir. Sit down and wait, please."

I met Tudor Petrov two months earlier when a delegation of Moldovan lawyers and police officials visited Vermont as part of Project Harmony's Community Connections program, which hosted varied delegations from several former Soviet republics. At that time I knew little of Moldova except that ownership of this small bit of territory had been long disputed by Romania and Russia. What is now Moldova had been part of the former Soviet Union since 1940. Because I spoke some Romanian, now the official language of this new republic, I was asked to serve as a host for a week. For me it was a chance to brush up on my Romanian, something I would need to do because I would be returning to Romania to teach at Babeş-Bolyai University for six months beginning in October.

I saw little of my guest during the days, when he was traveling the state meeting with Vermont's attorney general, police chiefs, and various states' attorneys, judges, and public defenders. In Soviet times Major Petrov would have been part of the KGB, although his role would be more analogous to the FBI here. He was a compact man of average height, with a round, unlined face, shortish brown hair turning to gray, large plastic-framed glasses, and a shy but ready smile.

Sitting on my front porch after his first day in Vermont, we talked of the changes overtaking Eastern Europe and the former Soviet Union. "Just a few short years ago, it would have been totally unbelievable that I—an Interior Ministry officer—would be sitting here with you now in 1998," he said. "Just unbelievable. But a whole new world is possible now. Anything is possible now!"

I would soon discover that Tudor's optimism is an exception in Europe's poorest country. But during those leisurely front porch conversations in the dog days of summer, I did not know this. We talked of food, faith, love, wine, and the messiness of democracy. Tudor possessed that same gentleness I had seen in many rural Romanians, not surprising given his people's origin. Like many Moldovans, he was proud of his Romanian roots and harbored considerable resentment towards his former Russian masters. And like most Moldovans, he was closely tied to the soil, finding the rural nature of Vermont instantly to his liking. "I feel so relaxed and at home here," he said repeatedly. "It's almost like being in the village where I grew up. "

One evening I mentioned that I would be in Romania beginning the following month. "Then, you *must* come to Chişinău," he said. "From Romania it is close, and I will introduce you to Moldova— and my kitchen, a true cultural exchange!"

*   *   *

Now, two months later, I'm checking my watch, wondering if the scheduled rendezvous with Tudor will take place on time. The customs official turns his attention to the mother, whom he apparently knows, and her two daughters. He does not check her bag. Meanwhile, Igor has driven the car over a pit, the car straddling it, next to the building. Through the window, I see two guards climb down and examine the underside of the car while he stands off to one side smoking and occasionally glancing at his watch. It is now nearly three o'clock, and inside it is hot, the air oppressively heavy and still. It smells of concrete, stale smoke, coffee, and cabbage. A few flies buzz listlessly around a flickering overhead fluorescent light. Large patches of dull gray paint have peeled away from the concrete walls and the ceiling like scabs, giving the room a wounded, leprous cast. The blue, yellow, and red flag of the Republic of Moldova hangs over the doorway with a color photograph of a coiffed and smiling President Petru Lucinschi hanging to one side. Less than ten years ago, I imagine, the red Soviet flag hung in that spot, along with a dour portrait of Mikhail Gorbachev. It is too late to visit that vanished imperium, but I hope to find echoes, at least glimpses, of the world that history has now swept away. The jackbooted border guards remain, as do the land and people, inheritors of a convoluted history.

Invaded and colonized by the Romans and subsequently by Huns, Bulgarians and Turks, this region, which is often referred to as Bessarabia by the Russians, has long been subject to cultural and military molestation by warring empires. After a brief golden age of independence in the thirteenth century, it was conquered by the Ottomans and remained under their control until the close of the Russo-Turkish war of 1806-1812. At that point, the eastern half of Bessarabia, what is now the Republic of Moldova, became part of the Russian empire. The western part would eventually become part of the new Romanian state in 1878, but until then it remained under Turkish control.

In 1918, Bessarabia unilaterally seceded from the Russian Empire and joined Romania, taking advantage of the chaos that followed the Russian revolution. However, the Kremlin never recognized that annexation. In 1940 it reclaimed that territory and together with a sliver of land on the eastern side of the Dniester river formed the Moldavian Soviet Socialist Republic.

This region became a killing ground during World War II, first as Romanian and German troops rampaged through the countryside, and then at the end as the Red Army drove them back across the Prut. Among those who suffered most were the Jews, two hundred thousand of whom were slaughtered by the Romanian Army in 1941.

Bitter over the Moldovan secession and allegiance to the fascist Romanians during World War II, the Soviets reasserted control here with particular harshness. They imposed Russian language and culture on every aspect of Moldovan life and were determined to stamp out the Romanian cultural identity through whatever means necessary. A million Moldovans were "relocated" to labor camps, coal mines, and factories in the Soviet Union. A corresponding number of Russians were moved into Moldova, taking positions of political, cultural, economic, and military leadership. Forced collectivization of the farms yielded widespread famine and death by starvation in the late 1940s.

After gaining its independence from Moscow following the breakup of the Soviet Union, the country felt the Russian boot again when Russian troops intervened in a brief civil war here in 1992, siding with ethnic Russian separatists in their efforts to form a breakaway republic in Transnistria, the region east of the Dniester River. The country is still partitioned, with most of its former industrial capacity and its sole power plant in the so-called Pridnestrovian Moldavian Republic (PMR). Several thousand Russian troops remain there as peace keepers, in defiance of international law.

A mere hundred miles away from those troops, I watch the Moldovan border guards climb out from the pit, their probes and mirrors having yielded nothing. They signal Igor to move the car, and we resume our trip. Here on the other side of the Prut there is even less traffic. We pass a few tractors and belching old military-gray Gaz trucks with bald tires. Along this road, the land, denuded of trees as far as the horizon, looks scruffy and neglected, as do the few small houses we pass. In a field to our right, a dead cow, bloated in the heat, lies near the road. Two large men in overalls stand away from it, covering their noses with handkerchiefs. I see a few pedestrians, old men and women mostly, waiting for busses in whatever shade they can find. We are in the middle of the hottest summer in thirty years, and the land looks parched. At one bus stop under the shade of a concrete portico, an old woman fusses over a sack of potatoes. A pink, black, and red scarf frames her sunken face. I do not see any dogs.

Beyond the first village, the Opel's engine begins to thump arhythmically. The car is losing power and then emits a harsh, metallic cough, backfires twice, and coasts to a stop by the side of the road. Igor sighs, grunts as he hauls himself out of the car, and opens the hood. Even with the windows down, it is roasting in the backseat without some air moving across us, and I soon join him outside. Alex, Igor, and I stare stupidly at the engine as if this will somehow unlock the mystery of this inopportune malfunction. Through the windshield I see the mother and her two children in the back staring blankly out the windows. The mother fans herself with a rolled-up newspaper.

A few minutes later, a rusty brown Soviet-era Lada passes in the opposite direction. It turns around, pulling off the road just ahead of us. The driver, a thin man wearing brown trousers and a yellow sport shirt, peers at the apparently defunct engine. He has a ruddy, cheerful face and wears thick glasses, which he now cleans with the front of his shirt. He and Igor begin to talk rapidly in Russian before a wad of bills changes hands. The Lada driver will take us to Chişinău.

"Come on," says the man. "Just put your bags in the trunk and let's go."

"What about our driver?" I ask.

He shrugs. "He wants to stay with his car. It is nothing to us," he says, my concern for a stranger seeming to annoy him.

A little while later we pass the crippled Chişinau/Iaşi bus, off to the other side of the road. At the back, the engine compartment lid is open and the rear panels are charred black. The bus appears to be full.

Despite the delays, I am dropped off in time to meet Tudor. It is still sweltering on this September afternoon, nearly ninety degrees in the shade. It is not a dry heat.

The bus station, a heavy, low-slung structure, sits in the middle of a teeming central market that sprawls across several city blocks. Just in front of the main entrance, Major Tudor Petrov waves to me. He must be broiling in his dark gray suit, I think, as we shake hands.

"Welcome to Moldova," he says, taking my bag. "I just now found out your bus was delayed indefinitely. How did you manage to get to Chişinau?"

I point to the parked Lada. "Five of us rode in from Iaşi."

Tudor frowns. "That could have been a dangerous thing to do," he says as we thread our way through the crowd. "I live only a short way from here. Let us get out of this awful heat."

The station is just a few blocks down from the main commercial street in Chişinău, Boulevard Stefan cel Mare, formerly Boulevard Lenin. For much of its three-mile length, it is lined with old oaks, and the buildings, many of them in the graceful Russian Provincial style, are set back from the sidewalks, behind the trees. I am surprised by the number of fancy shops selling high-priced clothing, jewelery, peek-a-boo lingerie, Italian, Swiss, and German kitchen appliances, and cosmetics. Ads touting Marlboro, Winston Light, Chanel, and Mercedes scream from shop windows and billboards. We pass an elegant sidewalk café, two waiters in starched white vests standing at the ready, while an after-work crowd of elegantly clad professionals sip beer and wine at linen-covered tables.

"This doesn't look like the poorest country in Europe," I say.

Tudor nods. "Everything you could imagine is for sale here in this city. *If* you have the money. The average Moldovan salary is three hundred lei a month, about thirty dollars, and a beer at such a place as this would cost half a day's wages. Looks, as they say, tell only a little part of the story. This is our own Potemkin Village."

Just down from the café is the stately Mihai Eminescu Theater, and then a hulking but oddly serene edifice that appears to have been built in the late 1940s in the Stalin Gothic mode. Tudor stops and points to the sign next to the main entrance. "This is where I work," he says. "It is close enough for me to walk home for lunch every day."

Two men in crisp, black military uniforms flank the large doors. They snap to attention and salute as we pass.

The Petrovs live three blocks farther down Stefan cel Mare in an old building on the fifth floor, shaded by the tall oaks that shield them from noise and the summer sun. It is an apartment of an upper-middle level member of the former state bureaucracy, a mark of privilege. The rooms have twelve-foot ceilings, plaster walls, and polished old parquet floors. French doors separate the spacious living room from the rest of the apartment. In the living room, a large couch occupies one wall, opposite which are two overstuffed chairs with a table between them. A new Panasonic TV sits in a corner by a large and almost empty bookcase. Photos of a young boy and girl hang on the walls.

Tudor's wife, Anna, is a pretty woman with red hair, friendly blue eyes, and an open, expressive face. She has a soft voice, as does her daughter, Rodika, who is seventeen and a senior in high school. She wears what seems to be the uniform of Eastern European girls everywhere: a T-shirt and artificially streaked skin-tight pegged jeans. Their son Serge is nine and we shake hands with grave formality.

It is very nice to be here in their kitchen eating roast chicken, fresh tomato and cucumber salad, and roasted potatoes, drinking some of the best wine I have had the pleasure of tasting. Our talk is lazy, deliberately light, as we discuss tomatoes, growing seasons, grapes, and the almost religious devotion Moldovans have for garlic—a devotion I share. A slight breeze now drifts through a large open window, but it is no match for the still-oppressive heat outside. Anna is apologetic. "This has been the hottest any of us can remember," she says. "At least we have the trees to shade us." Outside, grackles chatter and fuss, and I hear the sound of car horns and car engines muffled by the thick foliage between us and the street.

"We have a surprise for you," Tudor announces.

"Only, of course, if you are interested," says Anna.

"I'm interested in everything in Moldova," I reply.

They both smile. "Anna's sister Oxana is having her fortieth birthday tomorrow. It is a little party out in the *padura*, a typical Moldovan party, and we'd like you to come. You will see real life."

Rodika snorts. Anna flashes her a look.

"You will see a lot of cops," Rodika says, her top lip curling slightly. "Most of the guests will be police and their families."

"Your father is police and *he's* very nice, isn't he?" Anna says.

"Yes, he's very nice, but he's not *really* police, not *that* kind of police," she says with a shrug that suggests there is no more to be said on the matter. "He doesn't even carry a gun."

We gather in front of a nearby police station at ten the next morning. The women wear nice summer dresses, the men mostly slacks and short-sleeved shirts. Most carry huge bouquets of roses for Oxana. Four microbuses transport about forty of us north of Chișinău through sparsely populated and slightly more hilly terrain. Here the land seems more productive, and fields of potatoes, beets, and sunflowers spread out on both sides of the main road. We pass a large man-made lake just beyond the edges of the city and a neat apple orchard before climbing into more wooded terrain, with meticulously groomed second- and third-growth stands of birch and larch. After about an hour, we pull onto a side road and go for another two miles to a state park. Picnic tables with barbecue pits line the shore of a slowly moving river, along which fathers and sons, many in tattered straw hats, fish.

Just up from the river bank is a new, two-story white stucco house with a steep red-tiled roof. We are on the ground floor, where two rows of banquet tables span the thirty-foot length of the room. In the kitchen, five women are busy assembling platters of food for the tables: halved hard-boiled eggs garnished with bright red paprika; smoked sturgeon with lemon and parsley; tomato, feta, and olive salad—the tomatoes a deep, almost shimmering red, like hot coals; mushrooms in sherry and sour cream; cold pork schnitzels; sliced pickles; potato salad; and bright orange pickled carrots.

It is not yet time to eat, so Tudor and I go for a short walk down to the river. Although it remains hot, a breeze off the water brings some relief out here, where it is probably ten degrees cooler than in Chișinau. We pass a table of men in short-sleeved cotton shirts and shorts having a vigorous early lunch of bread, sausage, cheese, fish, and jugs of wine. They sweat heavily in the sun. One of them, a burly, smiling, florid-faced man with a mop of curly graying hair nods as we pass.

"That, by the way, is the head of the Communist Party of Moldova, Vladimir Voronin," Tudor says as we head back to the waiting celebration.

"Is he important now?" I ask

"Unfortunately, yes," he says. "And unfortunately, he will be our next president I think."

When we return, Anna and Oxana are already inside. The tables, now full with carefully arranged platters, are magnificent. I remember when I was a kid seeing pictures in *Soviet Life* of "typical holiday feasts," and this one perfectly recalls those old color shots. Issues of that magazine would appear intermittently in our public library during brief periods of thaws in international relations, and I would devour them with an intensity that baffled my parents.

In front of every plate are two bottles, one *apă minerală* (mineral water), one *Aroma* brandy. About a dozen large pitchers of white wine run the length of each table. At the head of mine, a stout man with short blond hair—a police captain, Anna tells me—seems to be the master of ceremonies. In a booming voice he shouts, "Sit. Sit down. Sit down, please! Today we celebrate Oxana's birthday. And today we welcome a visitor from America." The Captain holds up his glass of brandy and nods to me. "Everybody, fill your glasses and toast the birthday girl!"

Tudor leans over and whispers in my ear, "Empty your glass. It is insulting if you leave anything."

I empty it.

"Now, let's toast our American visitor," the Captain growls.

Tudor pours out more brandy; once again we drain the glasses. Then it is my turn. "Thank you very much. I am honored to be here with you all," I say in Romanian. Lifting the glass, I nod to Oxana: "For you, Oxana."

The Captain makes sure the glasses are kept full, and during the next hour, he pays particular attention to mine. At one point I stupidly put my hand over the glass, but he pushes it away. "You must learn to drink like a Moldovan," he says, with a vaguely sinister, peremptory tone. "Don't worry, we will teach you."

I imagine him looming over a prisoner who is tied to a chair. I imagine him impatiently flicking a riding crop against his jack-booted leg, leering at the captive. Eyes bulging, he screams, "You will drink. We have ways of making you drink!"

The platters of food, all superb, are finished within an hour, and people begin to file back outside. I have eaten much too much, and I have drunk far more than I am accustomed to. Following a narrow footpath beyond the sloping shores of the river, I find my way to a small pasture, where the sun-scorched grass crunches under my feet. I vomit violently into a thicket of sumac and then have a sudden and overwhelming urge to lie down beneath the haphazard shade of a stunted apple tree. The sound of squabbling crows is the last thing I recall.

The sun is noticeably lower in the sky when I open my eyes again. I look at my watch; I have been out for almost two hours. I get to my feet unsteadily and start walking, feeling better as the park comes into view. At least I am no longer nauseated. Never again will I eat or drink that much, I tell myself, relieved that I have at least survived my first encounter with what Moldovans proudly refer to as their "aggressive hospitality." As I cross a fence and approach the park house, I begin to smell roasting meat. The smell is faint at first, but it grows stronger as I rejoin the party in front of the house. No one, it seems, has noticed my absence. Off to the right, I see Tudor and Anna, who wave energetically. I wave back. The Captain, apparently, is also a pit-master and now presides over several grills, beneath which are glowing beds of applewood coals. Dozens of pork chops sizzle on metal racks. "What is this?" I ask as casually as I can, pointing to the cooking meat and hoping to hide my mounting horror. I am in no condition to eat again, but I don't want to insult my hosts.

The Captain shrugs and gives me a puzzled stare: "What is this? Supper, the main course. What did you think it was?"

As I retreat, he laughs unpleasantly. "You will learn to eat like a Moldovan!" he shouts after me. "Don't worry! We will teach you!"

A half-hour later, his faced flushed by the heat of the coals and no doubt by many glasses of brandy, the Captain again presides over the festivities. Platters of fragrant meat line the tables along with bowls of potatoes, cabbage, and more tomatoes.

"My God, another meal already," I say to Tudor, who shakes his head.

"No, not another meal. The same meal. This is just the main course."

What had preceded this, apparently, was merely a prelude. With a twinge in my stomach, I also note that new bottles of brandy are in front of each plate and the pitchers are again full, this time with red wine.

Flanked by Anna and Tudor, I give what I hope is a convincing smile as we lift our glasses once again. "Instead of just a toast to Oxana, this time I offer a song," the Captain says and begins to sing. I am stunned. His voice is beautiful. It is a rich, smooth, and pitch-perfect tenor, exquisite and unexpected. When he stops, he drains his glass. We all drain our glasses. I have no trouble draining mine.

Tudor loads up my plate with pork. "This is our national specialty, *costiță*, like your barbeque but not sweet. You will love it!"

I do, but as we eat, I think about Stalin's notorious late-night suppers, during which he would "invite" his inner circle to join him. In his autobiography, *Khrushchev Remembers*, Nikita Khrushchev offered vivid accounts of what he called these "interminable agonizing dinners." It was necessary but painfully difficult to keep up with Stalin's alcohol consumption; not to do so would have been an egregious affront to his Georgian hospitality, an affront, Khrushchev hinted, that could have had lethal repercussions. As Stalin's successor told it, night after night, the top leadership of the Soviet Union—Stalin, Khrushchev, the loathsome pederast and rapist Beria, Malenkov, Bulganin, among others—would eat and drink themselves into semi-consciousness before staggering off into the thin light of a Kremlin dawn.

Whatever plans the Soviets devised for the newly reacquired lands west of the Dniester could well have been formulated in such a drunken fog. Certainly the results, as far as the Moldovans were concerned, couldn't have been worse.

Later, after the meal is finished and the tables have been cleared away, the dancing begins. Having survived this long, I am now apparently okay in the eyes of the Captain, who grins lopsidedly at me from across the dance floor. There is no disco or Europop here: the tunes are strictly old-time folk, as are the dances, including a version of the *Gopak*, in which the Captain, like some crazed Energizer Bunny, now squats on his haunches and kicks out his heels. Thank God, I am not asked to do this.

ACROSS THE RIVERS

It is dark outside, but although the windows and doors are open, the room is still stifling. The heat, however, now seems oddly comforting, a joyous human heat full of energy, life, and reassuringly primal smells of sweat and skin. Leaning against the wall in a corner, I watch the dancers moving from circles to couples and back with practiced ease. I am feeling very lucky. In the country for little more than twenty-four hours, I have already been included in what is obviously a family affair, and for that I am grateful. This day has been a window into the private life of Moldovans, the life of kitchen conversation, feasting, dancing, and friendship.

This day has also been an expensive one, and I have no idea how it was financed. I try to squelch churlish thoughts of the Captain extorting money in shoeboxes, but I am not successful.

I do not discuss this with my hosts.

*　　*　　*

Casa Presei, a late-1960s concrete office building housing most of the print media of Chişinău, occupies a shady corner of Pushkin Street. Inside, the lobby is cool and dimly lit, a blessing considering the oppressive heat and the after-effects of Oxana's party the day before. It is one of those interesting legacies of the Soviet period. Still owned by the government, the building houses a variety of publications, some of them in opposition to the current regime of President Petru Lucinschi. I am here simply because it seems to be the best place to meet journalists, and I am trolling the hallways for new contacts. In a new place, it is often helpful to talk with reporters who can, depending on their political orientation, give me at least a sense of the local political, social, and economic dynamics.

About halfway down a long, dark corridor on the third floor, a slight man sits before a computer screen in a small office, the shades drawn against the insistent sun. A battered desk is at each end of the room, only a few feet separating the ends. An old fan clatters loudly, feebly pushing the air around. As I enter this room, he looks up, puzzled by my presence. His bearded face is dark and gaunt. Peering out from a pair of square-framed reading glasses, he blinks rapidly. "Yes, can I help you?"

I introduce myself.

He removes his glasses. "An American?" he says, switching to heavily accented English.

I nod.

"An American who speaks some Romanian and who even knows that Moldova exists?"

I nod again.

"Incredible."

He stands up and extends a hand. "My name is Nicolae Pojoga. Please, what is it that you want?"

"Just to talk. To have a coffee maybe and talk."

He nods slowly. "You are lucky because I am *very* good at both."

Behind Casa Presei in a shaded courtyard is a large outdoor restaurant. We sip thick espresso and smoke Astras, the local and wonderfully strong cigarette. Nicolae is both a photojournalist and a regular writer for several papers in the capital. He is, he tells me, one of the few ethnic Romanian Moldovans who also writes for the Russian language press.

"So, what do you want to know?" he asks.

"I'd like to get some understanding of the reality here."

He blinks at me.

"There is no reality here."

"Is it true that people are starving and eating their dogs? And selling their kidneys?"

Nicolae hesitates before answering. "Sometimes. I am sure of it. You must understand we are not a normal country. We are like a haunted house. The Soviet Union is dead, but it affects us all just the same. All our economy was geared to that, and our markets are still in the East. And we are still living off of that empire. Just look around you. All of our infrastructure is Soviet, including our brains. And *everything* is slowly falling apart—streets, water, health care, education—everything."

"So, what's going to happen here?" I ask, impressed by this man's exuberant gloom. "This sounds so pessimistic."

He nods and lights another Astra. "I am a journalist, not a clairvoyant. I think about this often, and I cannot have an answer except to say I see no future for us as an independent country. We are in some kind of horrible suspension between Romania, which has no desire to save us, and Moscow, which can surely destroy us in a second. We are an accident, an absurdity. How can you understand something like this? How can *anyone* understand this?"

We talk through much of the afternoon in the shaded courtyard, the hum of traffic not far away. I do not want to impose further on his time, but he dismisses that concern with a wave of the hand. "I finished my story just before you arrived," he says. "Besides, it's too hot to think. Let's go for a drink. I know the perfect place."

Nicolae's apartment building, 102 Dosoftei Strada, sits on a quiet street just a few hundred yards behind the old Orthodox Church in the center of Chişinău, overlooking the central flower market. He lives on the third floor with his wife Floarea and two young daughters, Ileana, seven, and Anica, three. It is, he tells me, a typical late-Soviet-era apartment, built in 1986 especially for journalists. After the collapse of the Soviet Union, the residents were basically given the apartments for a token payment. These structures are common throughout the former USSR: stacked prefabricated blocks with large expansion seams striating the exteriors of tile or painted concrete.

This apartment is spacious by old Soviet standards. It has an ample living room that doubles as a bedroom, a smaller bedroom where the children sleep, a bathroom, kitchen, small entrance hallway, and a balcony encased by windows off the living room. Several icons adorn what little available wall space remains. The apartment is dominated by books, which occupy every bit of wall not inconvenienced by a door or window. It is a polyglot collection of works by Russian, Romanian, French, Spanish, Latin American, and English writers: Turgenev, Tolstoy, Dostoyevsky, Gogol, Lermentov, Chekov, Kafka, Celan, Faulkner, Hemingway, Sartre, Voltaire, Eliade, Borges, Marquez, Shakespeare, Milton, Joyce, Solzhenitsyn, Dickens, Huxley, Orwell, Eminescu, and hundreds of lesser lights keep company on sagging shelves running from floor to ceiling. Thirty-five millimeter negatives hang from a clothesline running along one wall and above a cluttered and deeply scratched wooden desk covered by piles of newspapers, reporter's notepads, scraps of paper, scattered negatives, a few small stuffed bears, and a defunct Apple computer.

A cotton goose with half its tail chewed off lies across the keyboard, left there earlier in the afternoon by Anica, who now sleeps sprawled out on the couch, one arm flung over her head. Ileana practices arpeggios on an upright piano in the other room.

At forty-eight, Nicolae is strikingly gaunt, a function of his disposition, he says, rather than hunger. "I eat all the time, but I am a very nervous man, always smoking and drinking coffee," he explains. He looks Arabic, with his black hair just beginning to gray, full beard, dark olive skin, and a prominent, angular nose, long and bent just below the bridge. He could be frightening were it not for his eyes, which are deeply recessed, gentle and sad. A smile crosses his face as he looks at Anica, sleeping near him. "My three treasures," he sighs, "my three women who torment my existence."

Floarea, who is five years younger than Nicolae, works occasionally as a music tutor, but she does not work much. "I am here mostly with my children, and all of those," she says, pointing to the wall of books next to the couch.

"They drive Floarea crazy," Nicolae says. "'Get rid of these,' she tells me all the time." He says this with a playful whine. Floarea glares at him.

"Someday *I* will get rid of them," she says to me. "All these books. We can't eat books."

He follows her with his eyes as she leaves the room and then turns back towards me: "While we are on the subject of eating, I must ask you: How did you get to Chișinău?"

I tell him of the abortive bus ride and the Romanian train trip from Cluj-Napoca to Iași.

"Ah, then you took *trenul foamei*—the train of hunger."

"Yes," I say.

"Do you know why it is called *trenul foamei*?"

"I think so. Although it traverses all of Romania, it has no food service of any kind, for sixteen hours."

Nicolae takes out a bottle of clear liquid and two small glasses from a cabinet. "Yes, but there's another explanation, unfortunately. In the first years of the Soviet occupation, we were starving here. There was a famine that followed the forced collectivization after the war. My family, like all farm families, went through this. You cannot imagine what happened here. Half a million died, starved to death during this period. Half a million! And another half million deported to Siberia. People were desperate to leave. Risking their lives, thousands fled across the river and then hopped onto the roofs of the same train you came to Iaşi on, heading west into Transylvania. The Romanians used to call these refugees 'wires' and treated them very badly."

"Why did they call them wires?" I ask.

"For two reasons. They were so skinny—like wires. And because for each car someone had to be responsible to watch for overhead electric and telephone lines and warn the others to lie down. They would shout, 'Wires!' to alert the others. This was an incredible tragedy. If you want to understand Moldova, you have to understand a few things: you have to understand what kind of attitude the Romanians have towards us, what the Russians did to us after the war, how they tried to destroy our culture, turn us all into Russians. Yes, they have a beautiful culture also, and their literature and music are magnificent. But that is not the point. We have ours, too. You also need to understand what they are *still* doing to us, and for that you need to understand what happened in June 1992."

"You mean the civil war?"

"Exactly. I covered that abomination as a photographer. And now, it is a different—and worse—world across the river."

I have been aware of the so-called Pridnestrovian Moldavian Republic, also known as Transnistria, since its inception, having followed post-Soviet events carefully, and also having acquired some knowledge during Tudor Petrov's brief stay in my home. Like the residue of a bitter divorce, responsibility for the partition of the nascent Moldovan state and the ensuing spasm of violence depends upon who is telling the story. Secessionists in Tiraspol cast the civil war as a defensive one to preserve the Slavic identity of the Russians and Ukrainians who form the majority in this narrow strip that accounts for about 12 percent of Moldovan territory. Others, however, see it as something else entirely, a cynical exercise in power consolidation and public manipulation.

On the surface, the ethnic explanation is reasonable, and the early actions of the newly independent Republic of Moldova in 1991 accelerated mounting tensions between ethnic Slavs and ethnic Romanians. Proclaiming themselves "brothers with the Romanian people," some members of Moldova's new parliament urged reunification with Romania, much to the consternation of many living in the eastern part of the country in Transnistria. Many of those still saw themselves as citizens of the Soviet Union.

One of the new government's first actions was to proclaim Romanian the official state language, which certainly did nothing to refute the claims of the secessionists across the Dniester River. Raising the specter of a Moldovan state unifying with Romania, the former Communist leaders in Tiraspol, many of them the managers of huge state enterprises they intended to steal, orchestrated an effective campaign of fear leading to the outbreak of civil war. With the support of elite units of the Russian 14th Army division under the command of General Alexander Lebed—later a candidate for Russian president— they proclaimed independence from Chișinău. They would at least preserve what they had so far managed to hold on to, including most of Moldova's industry, vast underground reserves of aging wines and brandies, a thriving arms sector, and the sole power plant in the republic.

Who exactly fired the first shots is not certain, but from February through June of 1992, fighting along the Dniester River between Moldovan police and Interior Ministry forces and Transnistrian defense forces compelled at least 30,000 ethnic Romanians to flee Transnistria, and, depending upon the source of estimates, somewhere between 600 and 1200 people on each side of the river perished. Lebed's 14th Army's intervention on the separatist side ensured their success.

An agreement between Moldova and the Russian Federation in July ended the fighting and provided for deployment of a joint Moldovan-Russian-Transnistrian peacekeeping force, which remains in place to this day, along with a legacy of bitterness and distrust.

There is also another legacy, a toxic vortex of sophisticated organized crime. Corruption is endemic in all parts of the former Soviet Union, but it is particularly severe in the PMR, which according to Tudor Petrov belongs entirely to the Russian Mafia. "The president, Igor Smirnov, is mafiosi, his son is mafiosi," Petrov told me six weeks before as we talked late into the night on my front porch. "These people sell everything official for dollars: guns, petrol, wines, foods, cigarettes, steel, but very little ever gets reinvested in that so-called country. Most of it winds up in bank accounts abroad. When they've made everything they can, things will then collapse, but by then they'll be gone, along with their money. They will steal everything. The situation, and especially smuggling, is a big problem for us in Moldova, although some are getting rich because of it, you can be sure. Everything from gasoline and diesel to guns and stolen cars are involved. It is a bad and dangerous place. Believe me you do *not* want to go there."

Nicolae pours out two small glasses of perfectly clear țuică. He does this, as he does everything I have seen him do so far, slowly and with great care. Handing me a glass, he says, "This is excellent quality. It is from my village, and it is pure. Absolutely pure." He cuts a large garlic sour pickle into thin strips. He takes a sip, then a bite of the pickle. "The combination is wonderful, magical, what we call restorative."

He is right. The țuică is superb, better than any I have had in Romania, and the combination is wonderful. As I drink, I continue to think of Tudor's comments about Transnistria, about the PMR, which is a mere hour away by car.

"Do you go to Transnistria ever?" I ask.

Nicolae shakes his head. "No, never. Not since the war. I have thought about it a number of times. I should go, but I have not done it."

"Do you have any contacts there?"

He nods. "I have a friend, Larissa, who used to be in the police in Tiraspol, before the war, and she goes back and forth sometimes. She has friends there still."

"Is it a problem for you to go?"

"For me, no. People go back and forth all the time, but sometimes there are delays at the border."

"Do you want to go?"

Nicolae refills our glasses. "I think I do. It would be very interesting for me."

"Would I be able to go?"

"That is a very interesting question. Maybe. It depends on what happens at the border. I think the safest way is to go by bus or train. If you go by car, they will certainly want to see a sort of visa from you. Technically, as a foreigner you need a visa."

"How do I get one?"

"You cannot."

"I cannot?"

"No, you cannot."

"Why?"

"Because they do not exist."

WELCOME TO HELL
Tiraspol, 1998

The old rattletrap bus slows as it approaches a border that theoretically does not exist. The bus is full, mostly of old women either returning to Tiraspol or going to visit. Nicolae tells me these women have family on both sides of the new border and make this trip often. About a dozen soldiers with PMR armbands stand around sweating in dark green uniforms. The old green and red Soviet Moldavian SSR flag flies from a post in front of a couple of rusting trailers. We are at the border.

"Keep your head down, pretend you're sleeping," Nicolae whispers. "Just be quiet."

A soldier boards the bus and scans the interior, raking his eyes down both sides of the aisle. He stamps a paper and hands it to the driver, then steps down. The door clangs shut behind him.

"You cannot understand what a monstrous provocation this border is for us," Nicolae says. "It's an insult to see this: a border inside my own country. It is a cancer. These people on this bus, they have to endure this ritual humiliation every time they want to cross to see relatives or visit the graves of family. And why?"

Across the border, the road signs tell us immediately we are in another country, recognized or not. They are in Russian, peeling, and faded blue. In the city of Bendery, we pass a small war memorial, a tank with an eternal flame in front of it. Emblazoned on concrete walls lining the road are slogans in Russian: "We Will Survive!" "Faith in our Motherland!" "Together we are strong!" A tank under camouflage netting sits beside the main bridge crossing the Dniester, on top of which the PMR flag is defiantly displayed.

"It was a surreal existence, really," Nicolae says peering out the grimy bus window. "I actually commuted to the war every day, packing a lunch and hitching a ride from Chişinău. It was a very democratic experience. I was almost killed by both sides for the same reason: I was documenting this monumental idiocy."

As we cross the bridge, he continues. "I remember there being so many bodies just floating in this river—here right under us—and it was impossible to tell which side they died for."

About twenty minutes later, we approach what used to be an industrial showpiece of the Soviet Union, Tiraspol. "My god, just look at this place," he says slowly shaking his head. "It was not like this last time I was here." While traffic is certainly sparse on most roads in Moldova, at least in Chişinău it is often congested. Here in this urban center, the capital of the PMR, the roads are empty.

The bus deposits us on the main thoroughfare, Ulitsa Oktober 25, named after the Bolshevik revolution in 1917. Down the block, on top of a crumbling five-story apartment building, a large black dog paces nervously along the edge of the flat roof. It appears frantic, glancing down as it emits a high-pitched ululating howl.

"You know the myth of Cerberus?" Nicolae asks, pointing to the roof.

"Of course. It guarded the entrance to Hades."

"Exactly. Well, here we are."

Tiraspol seems almost spectral. Rusting cranes dominate the capital's skyline, looming like skeletal giraffes above unfinished apartment blocks that are already crumbling. The pavement is pock-marked with deep holes, the sidewalks dissolving from neglect. It reminds me immediately of Bucharest at the nadir of the Ceauşescu era in 1988 but even less cared for.

Most shops along this main street are dimly lit and carry goods no one could possibly sell anywhere else. The men's section of a downtown "department store" offers a rack of acetate shirts, a dozen badly made pairs of shoes, and eight identical blue double-breasted suits with labels in Russian reading "Made in the German Democratic Republic" sewn in the lining. Two stores down, a rank-smelling market offers plastic bags of macaroni, paper sacks of sugar, cloudy gallon jars of pickles that resemble fetal pigs, and a few quart jars of yogurt.

A woman in a dirty white smock applies a thick layer of lipstick as we enter. She looks up briefly, long enough to scowl at us from behind the counter. "This is all very nostalgic for me," Nicolae says, picking through emaciated chickens in a freezer beneath which a compressor rattles loudly. "This could easily be 1980. You want to know what it was like? Well, just look around, and you will have your answer."

A few new stores have sprung up incongruously like delicate flowers among the weeds, brightly lit, glitzy boutiques selling Western chic for hard currency. These offer cellular phones, French perfume, elegant dresses, German lingerie, and polar fleece jackets for $250 apiece. Through the window of one such place, a sleek young woman in a clinging dress dabs perfume from a tiny bottle onto one of her wrists. She sniffs it gingerly. A bored-looking Armani-clad man with a shaved head, Lenin-style beard and a massive gold watch stands next to her, a cell phone pressed to his ear.

On the street most of what little traffic there is consists of battered Russian Ladas and Moskvitches. But new Mercedes, BMWs, and SUVs line the curb in front of *Prikhlada*, an obviously new restaurant outside of which an array of signs—consisting of circles with diagonal lines drawn through them— offers pictographic instruction in etiquette: no guns, knives, grenades, shouting, or Molotov cocktails. Another curious sign, this one in English, reads "Face Control."

A war memorial to those who died in the Afghanistan and civil wars dominates the center of the city. Several hundred graves fill the back part of the park. "You need to see this," Nicolae says. We stare down at a photograph etched in a gravestone. It is a sweet face, unmarred by care and the toll of years. He gazes innocently back at us, we who are intruders on his solitude. The inscription under his picture reads simply "Leonid Tostenko: *1974-1992*."

Hundreds of similar markers dot the ground, many of them adorned by bouquets of freshly cut peonies and roses. Nearby, in the shadow of another old tank with a red star, a babushka in a tattered print dress stoops to sweep up a pile of newspaper and broken glass with a handmade broom.

A large statue of Lenin, thousands of which were gleefully dismembered following the collapse of the Soviet Union, gazes serenely towards those gravestones across the wide boulevard. There is something undeniably unsettling about this place, a place that seems to combine the worst elements of Communism with unbridled corruption, a place where the KGB still pounds on doors under cover of darkness and the press is rigidly censored. It is a time warp, a neo-Stalinist theme park, and here the trappings of Soviet hagiography remain. Massive billboard exhortations proclaiming the righteousness of the PMR, the Red Star, the Soviet Moldavian flag, the hammer and sickle, the strident propaganda, and the jackbooted police all seem like surreal, ghostly legacies of the dead imperium.

Nicolae scans the nearly deserted avenue, fixing his eyes on the large statue across the street. He blinks rapidly as if trying to gather fractured shards of recollection.

"For me, this is a trip back to the past, back to the old days, when the KGB could drag you out of the bed in the middle of the night because of what you thought," he says, pointing to a large sign displaying the hammer and sickle, beneath which floats a political slogan glorifying the sacrifices of the hero/worker. "Here this is still the Soviet Union, only now it's worse. Nothing functions here except the local mafia.

"It was oppressive in a way you cannot understand," he goes on, a quiet urgency in his voice as he lights another Astra. "My mind was always under attack. At least that was how I felt so much of the time. Always I felt the pressure here, right here," he says, pointing to his temples.

While he was not an official dissident, his relationship with the authorities had been tenuous, and in 1980, he crossed a line. Sent to cover the Moscow Olympics, Pojoga photographed a number of celebratory moments in Chişinău, including scenes of bleary-eyed, obviously drunk young men brandishing beer bottles and flashing the victory sign. Worse still, the pictures somehow got published. There were repercussions.

"I was invited for an interview with the KGB," he says as we head away from the tombstones. "They were furious. They could not understand why I took such pictures during this moment of Soviet triumph, the Olympics. It was, they said, slander of the State. I told them I was simply doing my job. In the end, they suggested I would do better in a different job, and as what they imagined to be punishment, they assigned me to be the photographer for the national theater right in Chişinău. It was the best gift they could have given me. In some ways it was the happiest time in my life."

Still, the pressures of conformity were constant irritations, as was the realization that the authorities could change his well-being at any point they wished. And now, despite the removal of material security, he dismisses any suggestion that he was perhaps better off then. "It is my life now. Not the State's. I am a man, not some kind of child who needs to be constantly watched. At least there is a chance now—sometimes—to be a real journalist, to be free of those kinds of chains."

Those kinds of chains are not hard to find here across the river. Our next stop is to talk with a woman with whom Nicolae worked during the Soviet times. "She was a total idiot and therefore very successful in the Soviet Moldavian media," he explains as we approach the Olvia-Press Agency, which occupies a small building tucked quietly away from Ulitsa Oktober 25. Olvia-Press is the official voice of the PMR, and here, according to its director, Svetlana Antonova, you can get the real story, the truth unmolested by foes of President Smirnov's regime and the Pridnestrovian Moldavian Republic.

Antonova is a large-boned woman in her fifties. Incipient jowls lend a vaguely basset hound quality to her face, which is crowned by a thick helmet of luridly dyed blond hair. While we are speaking with her in a sparsely furnished but roomy office, four men with shaved heads pace the room, glaring at Nicolae and me through a veil of Marlboro smoke. One of them sits on a windowsill and exhales from his nostrils as he watches us. I have seen this act before, in Romania. Have they all studied the *James Bond Guide to Villainy*? I want to direct a few questions to this man. I want to say, "Excuse me, Comrade, but why do you think exhaling smoke from your nose is going to frighten me? Where did you learn that adults are terrified by such things? Do you realize how stupid you look?"

Instead, I light an Astra, inhale deeply, stare back, and exhale through my nose.

Svetlana Antonova regards Nicolae warily, then sends a tight, quick smile in my direction. "Everything you hear about us from outside is a lie," she says, lighting a cigarette and exhaling through her nose.

"So where do I get the facts?" I ask.

Antonova glances down at the conference table. "Here. Here you can get the facts."

With bland assurance, she tells me that the PMR—in stark contrast to Moldova—has a stable economy. This, despite the obvious fact that the official currency, the "Cupon Ruble," is regarded even locally as a cruel joke with the inflation rate far outstripping that of Moldova, whose currency is remarkably stable. That stability, however, reflects a sociologically devastating reality: about one-third of the population, mostly women, work in Western Europe, often illegally, and send home about $100 million each month. About the same percentage from the PMR is thought to be in Russia illegally, also working.

"We have declared our independence economically. We have gone in different directions and have maintained the former system of government ownership." Antonova smiles broadly as she continues this interesting lesson in economics. "We, unlike Moldova, have no foreign debt."

She pauses, presumably for dramatic effect, and glances at Nicolae. "We have survived alone, like wolves in the wilderness," she says, a slight quaver in her voice. "We have not received *any* help from the international community. Do not insult us with talk about reunification! Why should we be burdened with Moldova's mistakes and disastrous attempts at reforms? We are not eager for so-called Western reforms. That is why we are targets and why our government has the ability to help keep our enterprises going. Our economy is the most socially oriented among the former republics of the USSR," she states proudly. "Unlike in Moldova, *our* retired people get their pensions on time, and all of the glorious Soviet social programs remain intact."

Any attempt to elicit hard facts about those glorious Soviet social programs is futile. Such figures are "closed information," Antonova insists. Also "closed" are any defense budget figures and statistics on public health and crime. As far as international assertions of mafia dominance go, she waves her hand dismissively. "Such problems exist everywhere in the former Soviet Union. If you want to talk about corruption, I suggest you go talk to the police."

Antonova bristles over suggestions that human rights violations are common in the PMR, and that the press is tightly controlled. Her upper lip lifts briefly in a canine snarl after I ask about KGB intimidation, rigged elections, and strict control of the press, all thoroughly documented by a recent United Nations Human Development Report. She shakes her head angrily. "More propaganda, more lies!"

She stands abruptly, walks towards the door and then turns to face us. "I do not have time for any more of this conversation," she says, spitting out each word. "You must now please excuse me."

Outside, we both take a deep breath. "Oh my God, what a very lovely interview," Nicolae says as we head back toward Ulitsa Oktober 25. "What a beautiful woman! What a very nice experience for an American journalist! I think I am going to be sick."

MY GOD, WHAT HAVE WE DONE?

Tiraspol, 1998

Among the residents of the PMR are nearly three thousand Russian troops, many housed in what was formerly the headquarters of Lebed's 14th Army division. Behind a rusting green iron gate, that headquarters now looks more like a slum. Many of the five- and six-story buildings are abandoned, the windows shattered, relics of the recently departed Imperium. Behind the walls, piles of rusting construction machinery, garbage, and stripped automobiles line the rutted roads. Other buildings remain functional, including barracks and maintenance sheds for the tanks, armored personnel carriers, and other mechanized infrastructure to support what is left of more than fifteen thousand troops originally stationed here.

Tiraspol had long been a vital military outpost, for both the Russian Empire and then the Soviet Union. Since World War II, this region was home to the Red Army's Southwestern Front Command, the launching point for a blitzkrieg into southeastern Europe should war have broken out. Such an invasion would have attempted to smash through NATO defenses and push southward to Athens. What remains of that force has been downgraded to an "Operational Group," but Nicolae isn't interested in semantic distinctions. Like all

Moldovans, he regards these soldiers as illegal occupiers, as does the international community.

But he also understands that part of the reason for their continued presence lies fifty miles to the north of Tiraspol, on a Russian army base in the town of Colbasna. "There is a huge problem in Colbasna," he says as we pass the military compound on Ulitsa 25 Oktober.

And a dangerous one, too: forty-four thousand metric tons of weapons, some dating back to World War II, are stored here. Most of this materiel goes back to the 1970s and 1980s, and enough remains to fill over twenty-five hundred railway cars. The Russians have removed some of the more unstable armaments, but what remains is scary enough. Large numbers of shoulder-fired anti-aircraft missiles, stockpiled ammunition, tens of thousands of Kalashnikovs, thousands of pistols, anti-tank weapons, mortars, and grenades—all highly portable. Russian control of these armaments is a subject of concern because many in Europe suspect that some of those arms have also been supplied to forces in Transnistria who have actively intervened in regional conflicts well beyond their own borders. In 1994, PMR Ministry of State Security troops participated in fighting on the side of Russian-backed Abkhazisans in Georgia, sent troops to fight on the Rutskoi-Khasbulatov hard-liner side against Yeltsin in Moscow during the 1993 standoff in the Russian Parliament, and are alleged to have aided Serbian operations in both Bosnia and Kosovo.

Tiraspol has long insisted that the ammunition and weapons left in Transnistria when the Soviet Union fell apart belong to them and are reportedly asking $1 billion in compensation, a figure Moscow has rejected outright. Also problematic is the PMR's insistence that it needs Russian troops stationed on its soil to guarantee against a resumption of the civil war, an event most observers believe to be highly unlikely. The Russians also point to a problem with Ukraine, which insists that Moscow pay it millions in transport fees to allow a Russian evacuation of ammunition and weapons across its soil, the only reasonable route out of Transnistria back to Russia.

Some of the remaining Russian soldiers are also serving as part of the peacekeeping force set up at the end of the 1992 fighting. Although not a shot has been fired for the past six years, they remain, closeted behind barracks gates when not manning a number of points along the border with Moldova proper. They wait for the chance to go home. For whatever reasons and whatever excuses, they, along with the rest of the Russian troops, remain on what is internationally recognized as Moldovan soil until the Kremlin decides otherwise.

I am lucky to have the apparently unheard-of opportunity to meet two of these Russian peacekeepers, Major Ghennady Sokolov and his wife Natalia, a non-commissioned officer, in their Tiraspol apartment. Given the sensitivity of their roles here and the no-doubt tight constraints under which they operate, I cannot understand why they would consider this meeting with an American and a Moldovan journalist. Perhaps they received authorization, but both Nicolae and I very much doubt it. The answer, Nicolae surmises, is his friend Larissa's long friendship with the Sokolovs. She has apparently vouched for Nicolae's integrity as a *blagorodnyy chelovek*, an honorable man. I keep in mind Nicolae's comments that, for Moldovans, the border with PMR is a painful provocation. I will now, it seems, be able to see that border as it appears to people on the other side.

The Sokolovs have a pleasant apartment just blocks from the main compound where they are officially stationed as part of the peacekeeping force. It is a typical Soviet apartment, and in this typical Soviet living room, three walls are covered with huge blown-up photographs of rustic Russian landscapes. One features a log cabin nearly buried after a winter storm, the surrounding hemlocks heavily laden with snow. Another depicts a shepherd walking with his flock alongside a river. On another, the Mir space station glows dramatically against the black backdrop of space. Nostalgia is visually palpable.

With close-cropped gray hair, a neatly trimmed moustache, and piercing blue eyes, Sokolov looks the part of a career soldier, as does Natalia, a compact, fit woman with a wide, expressive mouth and alert green eyes. They both say they are resigned to remain far from home, serving on a peacekeeping force that does little but safeguard what is internationally regarded as an illegal status quo.

Between bites of delicious chocolate cake, instant coffee, and homemade sherry, Sokolov offers a justification for continued Russian presence. "All people want here is what people want any-where—to live in peace, to have a normal life. They don't want to be part of Romania," he says.

The likelihood of that union is scoffed at both in Romania and in Moldova. Romania is in no position economically to absorb an even poorer Moldova, and the government in Chişinău is not about to surrender its authority to its ethnic cousins in Bucharest. Having at least nominally thrown off the yoke of the Kremlin in 1991, it is not eager to wear another made in Bucharest. This belief persists, nevertheless, and has been a powerful tool in fueling the current impasse.

"But isn't this is a dead argument?" I ask.

Sokolov's eyes narrow as he shakes his head emphatically. "I don't think so. The issue is still here, it's just in the shadows. Nobody seems to be able to resolve this problem. It is crucial there be an acceptable definition of autonomy for the Transnistrian region, and these people, on both sides, cannot do this. Just a lot of talk but not much work."

Natalia waggles a finger at her husband. "The politicians will just talk us all to death. I despise their talk, talk, talk. And tell me, please, when will this mess be resolved? When?"

Sokolov pats his wife's hand. "Only when both governments collapse and Moscow says we can come home: neither can survive this way. The living standard here and across the river is poor and getting worse fast. It must all collapse before anything really changes. Until then, nothing will change. *Nothing.*"

Sokolov spits out *nothing* like a curse—*Nichevo*—and I am surprised by the bitterness in his voice, a bitterness etched on both of their faces. They are contemptuous of Russian President Boris Yeltsin and their former commander, Lebed. "Do not talk to me about Yeltsin," Natalia snaps. "He is the one who allows this stupid situation to continue. And Lebed? Where is *he* now? I do not find him in Tiraspol, except for his photograph in a shop window. He is back in Russia running for president, flying around in helicopters while we are stuck here. He has abandoned us. Like everyone else."

Sokolov nods slowly. He leans forward, glances at Nicolae, and continues. "With all due respect to my Moldovan guest, I will say this: Transnistria has *always* been part of the Soviet Union and of the Russian Empire before that. This is, in that sense, a natural entity, a natural division. This land east of the Dniester was never part of Romania or what she claimed east of the Prut river. Never. So I can understand the fears of the populace here. When this was part of the Soviet Union, there was no problem for them, but now, until this is resolved, they are afraid. I can also tell you that having Moldova—and by extension Transnistria—part of NATO would never be acceptable to Moscow. Romania they will have to accept, but here, no. They cannot let that happen."

"Why should Russia care? The Cold War is over," I say. "What is the problem?"

"The problem is four hundred years of history. This is our backyard, our near abroad, and it is of vital strategic importance to us. Speaking as a military man, I can say Moscow has a *very* serious interest in how this problem is resolved."

"Then why is it not resolved?" I ask.

Sokolov shrugs. "That is a question I cannot answer. It is not for us soldiers to wonder about such things. I just know that we are stuck here patrolling this security zone. Okay, I can accept that. I am a soldier and being a peacekeeper is honorable work. But nobody here wants another war, on either side. Nobody. But we keep patrolling. For how long must this go on? We have no money, nothing for my son, nothing for his future. And there is no housing for any of us back home in Russia. At least here we have food and a roof over our heads." He turns towards Natalia. "We have no home to go to. We have only this here, living like exiles."

Natalia barks out a clipped laugh. "Exiles who do what we are told, like soldiers everywhere. Maybe someday the politicians will tell us we can go home."

On my way out, Sokolov takes my arm. His grip is surprisingly gentle. "This is all such a shame," he says. "For everybody. The only hope left in my life is when I walk into the apartment and see my son. I pray he will have a future, but I cannot see it from here. The old Soviet Union had problems, yes, but *nothing* on earth yet devised worked better for so many people as the former USSR. Now look at what we have. My God, what have we done?"

*   *   *

Nicolae and I are quiet as we walk towards the station. Few cars are on the street although it is only just a little past eight o'clock. A truck carrying troops, either PMR or Russian, rattles past us in the gloaming, belching out a thick plume of diesel smoke. We can smell it long after the dim taillight disappears around a corner.

"What do you think of our visit?" I finally say, breaking a silence that feels uncomfortable. I have been wondering what it was like for him to sit down with a man who is, in effect, the enemy.

"Well, I am sure Sokolov is not saying what he knows is the real situation," he says.

"Why are you so sure?"

"Because he is not a stupid man. I am sure his bitterness is real, but the other nonsense, no. All of this tragic stupidity is about only one thing, really."

"I thought this is supposed to be very complicated."

Nicolae fishes out two Astras as we walk. I take one.

"It is. You are right. Very complicated. Money is always complicated. Too many people are getting rich from this situation, here, in Moldova, in Ukraine, and especially in Russia. Smirnov's family controls everything here, all of it, and they have very influential friends in the Kremlin."

We pass a wall on which is painted a large sign. In the middle are a hammer and sickle and a clenched fist raised in defiance. Above it is written in large letters "PMR: Together We Are Strong!" I think of gang graffiti with a certain grim amusement.

Nicolae stops and stares intently at the painting on the cement wall. He shakes his head. "I was very curious to know how I would feel visiting this man. But now, I am relieved."

"Why?"

"Because sadness is better than hatred, and I think Sokolov is probably a good man, and an unfortunate one, like most of us—caught in someone else's game. Welcome to our great post-Soviet reality. There is no more evil empire, no more workers' paradise. But we still have paradise. If you are a criminal."

ANATOL PHILIPOVICH

Tiraspol, 2000

The fax from Tiraspol arrives on a Friday, just at the end of my five-day seminar for State University of Moldova students at the Independent Journalism Center in Chişinău. Through contacts made during my first visit to Chişinău two years earlier, I have been working with fourth-year journalism students, delivering an intensive seven-hour daily course in media ethics.

Nicolae, with whom I am staying, is amazed by the fax. "A genuine artifact!" he exclaims, shaking his head in wonder as he leafs through the itinerary. "Look at this—here, on page two: 'spontaneous meetings with average citizens.' This is priceless! Something from a time capsule. Only a true Soviet man could send such a document."

Before my return to Moldova, I had emailed Nicolae suggesting he join me for another adventure in Transnistria, but this time both of us would be legal. I had asked him for any contacts he might have in Tiraspol, anyone who could possibly open some doors while we were there. He knew of a part-time journalist, a fierce critic of the Smirnov regime in Tiraspol, who could not publish in the tightly controlled media of the PMR. His weekly column thus found its way to a Russian-language weekly in Chişinău for whom Nicolae occasionally worked.

Although he had never met Anatol Philipovich Platitzyn, Nicolae knew a little about the man through mutual friends. Like many Russians who have settled in Tiraspol, Platitzyn is retired military, a former colonel in military intelligence. He also had actively supported the separatists during the civil war eight years ago. He quickly turned against the new regime he had helped to establish, however, when it became clear that President Igor Smirnov and his cronies were thoroughly corrupt, authoritarian, and deeply allied with the Russian mafia, if not part of it.

Nicolae had explained to Platitzyn that I was a freelance journalist who wanted an accurate picture of the PMR, nothing less and nothing more. The former colonel quickly wrote back offering to facilitate a full week in the outlaw republic for $400—all expenses paid for two. He would be facilitator, host, and tour guide should we wish. Most importantly, he said he could provide something neither of us could on our own: official access.

Via his fax, still warm in our hands from printing, he has provided an itinerary worthy of the former Soviet Union's official tourist agency, Intourist, which was notorious for offering rigid, inflexible travel experiences. A portion from the itinerary reads:

Sunday, 21 May, 2000

7:30: Departure from Kishinev (Chişinău)

8:30-9:30: Filing visa documents at the border customs control office near the village of Varnitsa.

10:00-12:00: Participating in a religious service of the Pentecostals in Tiraspol.

12:00-13:00: Christian meal.

14:00-17:00: A visit to the Pyatro-Nyamtsky Orthodox Christian monastery. Monastery meal included.

17:30-19:00: A walk through the central part of Tiraspol city.

19:00-21:00: A meeting with the representative of a small and average business in Tiraspol.

21:00-22:00: A walk along the Dniester river bank

22:00: Return to apartment.

ANATOL PHILIPOVICH

Monday, 22 May, 2000

8:30-9:30: Breakfast in the apartment

10:00-12:00: Meeting the publishers of *Dniesterovskaya Pravda* newspaper

12:30-14:00: Meetings with the director of Moldovska School N 20

14:00-15:00: Lunch at the Hotel Druzhba

15:00-16:30: Meeting with director of the Republican Blood Bank

17:00-21:00: Touring the city at night

By Saturday evening, Nicolae's mood has grown distinctly gloomy. We are in his living room thumbing through his photographs of the fighting eight years earlier. He hands me a print of a man jumping out of the passenger seat of a truck. "He was already half out of the door when the shutter clicked," Nicolae says. "He probably died before he hit the ground, hit by a sniper from that building you can see at the edge of the frame." In what I have come to know is a gesture of distress, he takes off his glasses and pinches both sides of the bridge of his nose. "Part of me is still in that truck, I think."

"You don't have to go," I say.

Nicolae shakes his head. "No, it will be good for me to go. I haven't been back since our little invasion two years ago. Anyway, I need to go, if only to see what's happening. It is a very strange program he has arranged. I appreciate it from an anthropological perspective."

I wonder what it will be like for him to be with Platitzyn, a man who actively contributed to the partition of Moldova, a man figuratively, at least, at the trigger end of the separatist guns. He nods as I ask him this.

"That is very interesting," he says, lighting up another Astra. "If we never talk to our enemies, if we never understand them and if they never understand us, we stay enemies. We see clearly where that leads. I would like to understand, if only to be able to move beyond this terrible point. I want to get outside of myself. It was all so pointless, so tragic, this stupid war, and humans did this—people like me and Platitzyn."

*   *   *

A car arrives for us at precisely seven thirty on Sunday morning outside Nicolae's apartment. A tall, burly man slowly extracts himself from the passenger seat of a 1984 orange Mercedes sedan and lumbers toward us, limping slightly on his right leg. He wears a gray rumpled suit, blue shirt, and a dark red tie. His longish sandy-gray hair neatly combed back from his forehead and sharp blue eyes give him a slightly boyish air despite his sixty-three years and the deep lines in his face. In the morning light, a spider web pattern of tiny blood vessels in his cheeks and the puffiness beneath his eyes are clearly visible.

For the next five days, Anatol Philipovitch Platitzyn and Sasha, his driver who regards him with basset hound-like devotion, will constantly be with us: our friends, facilitators, protectors, and jailers.

As we head out of Chişinău towards the de facto border, Platitzyn, turning around to face us in the back seat, tells us what he hopes we will see. His voice is a low baritone—rumbling and vaguely assaultive, a voice accustomed to being heard. It is not a voice for lullabies. "I want you to get the real picture of this place," he says. "The real story is very complicated, not as simple as the Europeans and Americans would like to believe. Keep an open mind, please."

It is early May, and the countryside we pass looks lush. Fields of sunflower and alfalfa spread out to the distant hills, most of which are stripped of their forests. We pass through a few small villages of stucco houses with asbestos-tiled roofs, bright red geraniums gracing many of the window boxes. The houses sit tucked behind iron fences, their large gates mostly open. Behind many of them lie vegetable gardens and a few outbuildings for chickens and pigs. On this Sunday morning traffic is sparse, consisting of mostly a few groaning, belching trucks, rattling tractors, and the odd Lada.

Within an hour, we have arrived at the makeshift border. We pass a Moldovan checkpoint, and then pull up in front of what looks like a converted cargo container. A jackbooted soldier with a PMR insignia on his sleeve, a hammer and sickle on his cap, and a Kalashnikov draped over his shoulder glances down at the car.

Platitzyn takes my passport and Nicolae's identity card and with a grunt climbs out onto the curb.

Sasha watches us through the rear view mirror, a look of vague concern in his eyes. He is a squat man of about forty with liquid, bovine eyes and a protruding lower lip, which gives him the look of someone on the verge of tears.

Platitzyn returns a few minutes later and hands me back my passport. "You are now my responsibility," he says, leaning again over the back of the front seat. "This is not a healthy place for you. This can be a dangerous place for me, and I know what I'm doing. You haven't any idea."

We soon cross the bridge at Bendery, atop which still flies the green and red PMR flag. As we drive through town, slogans festoon walls and gates by the roadside: "The PMR will triumph!" "Onward to a better future!" "Yes we can!" "Glory to the Workers!" I am again surprised to see the hammer and sickle, but this odd place of only 650,000 souls is certainly not the Soviet Union—despite the apparent yearning for its return. For one thing, religion is freely practiced, as a visit to Mihail Carpovich Ceban's Pentecostal congregation clearly demonstrates.

In Tiraspol, 91a Ulitisa Gogol is remarkable for several reasons. It is new and compared to the other houses on the street, large. Also notable are the approximately eighty pairs of shoes laid out in neat rows by the front door on this warm spring Sunday morning. They are shoes of all sizes and varieties: boots, sandals, dress shoes, women's pumps, and clogs. Most are badly worn, some worn out and crudely stitched back together.

During Soviet times what is happening inside this house would have been punished harshly by imprisonment or internal exile: now Pentecostal leader Ceban and his congregation meet openly in a large room on the second floor of this new house. Most of the money needed to build it, as well as a new religious center under construction a few blocks away, comes from abroad, and much of that from Pentecostal groups in the southern United States.

Ceban, a short, rotund man with spectacles and thinning black hair that curls around his white shirt collar, greets Platitzyn with a big smile, a hug, and the customary Russian kiss on both cheeks.

The service is about to begin, he tells us, and leads the way up the stairs to a large, sparsely furnished room. The walls are bare save for unfinished pine wainscoting and black-and-gold-striped wallpaper. One bare light bulb dangles from the ceiling. Beneath it, men, women, and children sit on simple pine benches facing a bare podium. They are neatly dressed, the men in dark trousers and clean shirts, the women in long dresses. Nicolae tells me that as an Eastern Orthodox Christian, this visit is problematic, as would be any visit to a religious service not Orthodox. I am uncomfortable for other reasons. Among these fervent believers, I am an interloper, an agnostic, and an obvious foreigner, but they do not seem to mind. Ceban, in fact, asks the congregation to welcome us in their hearts before beginning his homily. Then a young man strikes a few chords on an electric piano, and the congregation begins to sing in jagged harmony. Although it is sung in Russian, there is no mistaking the melody of this hymn: "What a Friend We Have in Jesus." Directly under the bare light bulb, a cadaverously thin old man with watery eyes clutches a handkerchief with both hands as he sings, eyes turned upward, tears streaming down cheeks riven with deep lines.

Nicolae and I, who have hugged the wall by the door, leave as unobtrusively as possible and walk out into the warm sunlight behind the house, where a large garden about seventy feet by seventy feet fans out to neighboring fences. No land is wasted; every available inch is cultivated. Ceban's garden is already full of spinach and lettuce, with peas, chard, broccoli, peppers, and green beans coming along nicely. From one small lean-to, a pig grunts contentedly and behind a rusting fence, eight chickens peck the ground.

"They think you are some rich American who will help them," he tells me, lighting up another Astra.

"Why on earth would they think such a thing?" I ask.

"Because I am afraid Platitzyn has told them this. Ceban said something to me as we went up the stairs about your being from the church in America. I told him he was mistaken, that you were a journalist, not a church person. He seemed surprised."

After the service we enjoy "a Christian meal"—an item on Platitzyn's itinerary for us today. With Nicolae translating from Russian, Ceban wants to know what I will write. We are eating vegetable soup with sour cream, brown bread, and potatoes as I try to explain that I will write about what I see.

"Then you will write about a miracle," Ceban says emphatically. "Because this new house is proof of the power of prayer. Twenty years ago, we held prayer meetings in a secluded part of the forest in a village about twelve kilometers away from here. Any of us could have gone to jail for what we did, especially because we are Pentecostals. Now, look at us. This house was built with money from the congregation, but mostly from money from your country, from Mississippi! All of this from the power of our prayers. If only we could have another fifty thousand, we could finish our community center, which would provide us with a clinic and a Sunday school too."

An hour later, an ingenious ferry takes us across the silt-brown Nistru away from the city. Nothing powers the steel platform but the currents beneath us. A cable guides the boat the few hundred yards to a steep landing on the other side. Kids ride this ferry for free, and they now dive off into the middle of the river and try to scamper back onto the barge.

Old excursion boats hug the far bank, the red and blue hulls now dissolving slowly along the shoreline. Ten years ago, holiday-goers packed these vessels for daylong joy rides along part of this serpentine and often lethargic river that has seen so much carnage during the past sixty years. Now the deck railings are red with corrosion, and vertical striations of rust, like dried blood, plunge towards the muddy water.

Nicolae stares at the river, frowning as he peers into the brown soup. "So many bodies," he says, his soft voice barely audible in the wind.

I am again struck by this man's gentleness, something I don't expect from a photojournalist specializing in war zones. He has none of the swagger, none of the braggadocio, and when I point this out to him, he smiles sadly. "We are the witnesses, that's all," he says, and looks again into the water.

Through the years, many bodies have floated here. Just beyond the bank we are slowly approaching, thousands of German troops were killed and tens of thousands captured by the advancing Red

Army in August 1944 as it chased them back across the river, pushing them westward out of the Soviet Union and reclaiming all of Moldova in the process. Excepting a nearby battle monument, no evidence remains of that pivotal August battle.

Once the ferry has tied up, the Mercedes lurches up a steep, corrugated iron ramp to the road above. The tires spin and shriek before catching a grip. Traveling now along a narrow country road back towards Bindery and Moldova proper, we pass lines of men, women, and children along the road, the same road perhaps that those thousands of retreating Germans trod on their lethal retreat. This, however, is a leisurely procession, some on bicycles, but most on foot, many carrying small bouquets of peonies. They, like us, are headed to Noul-Neamţ monastery in Chiţcani. As monasteries go, this one is relatively new, but the feel and look are timeless. It was founded in 1861 by monks from Romania, and the compound took shape slowly over the next fifty years. Most of the buildings here were erected in the early twentieth century, including the five-story gate and bell tower. It is primarily a training seminary for hundreds of young men who will become priests in the Romanian branch of the Orthodox Church. To those approaching the huge wooden doors at the base of the bell tower, it is a blessed oasis of serenity and hope. To the regime in Tiraspol, it is an irritant, an outpost of the despised Romanian culture in their backyard.

Outside these walls in the nearby village of Chiţcani, numerous cases of beatings, rapes, and murders of ethnic Romanians by government thugs were reported between 1992 and 1997. More than forty people were victimized, and a local militiaman investigating several of these incidents was found hung at the site of one of the crimes. The Smirnov government vehemently denies any involvement in these incidents and brands all such allegations as Moldovan and Romanian "provocations."

As we enter through massive wooden doors nearly twelve feet high, a young prelate in simple black Orthodox garb walks briskly towards us, beaming a wide-open, honest smile in our direction. Beneath a crowned cap, his long dark hair is tied back in a ponytail, and with his full beard and simple cassock he could have stepped out of a Tolstoy novel. Father Paisie, the spiritual leader of this monastery, embraces Platitzyn and then looks at Nicolae and me. "Welcome," he tells us in Romanian, his eyes twinkling. We are ushered into a small, darkly wallpapered anteroom that manages to be both Spartan and comfortable. Paisie speaks briefly with Nicolae and leaves for a moment.

When he returns, he is with a tall, balding man in a white shirt and trousers. Elegant in his simplicity, Stefan is the *majordomo* within the monastery and will escort Platitzyn and me to its famous wine cellars. While we are thus occupied, Nicolae, presumably, will have his soul cleansed of the morning's Pentecostal visit.

We descend a steep stone stairway into a network of stone-vaulted chambers, and then the vinegar twang of fermenting grapes hits us. Platitzyn inhales the cool air deeply and smiles. Rows of oak casks flank us on all sides, and Stefan gestures for us to follow in the dim light. Behind us a young acolyte, a boy of maybe twelve, descends with a tray containing glasses and a plate of bread and crackers. He is pale, unsmiling, servile, and the effect is for me unsettling. "Just in case," Stefan says in heavily accented English, pointing to the food.

The monks here, along with a convent affiliated with them just beyond the border in Moldova proper, grow most of what they eat. That includes all meat, flour, grain, potatoes, vegetables, eggs, berries, and fruits, including, of course, grapes. All the wine here is produced from grapes grown either here or in the convent.

Stefan, Platitzyn, and I sample four varieties of red wine from the huge casks that are now ready for drinking: Cabernet and the regional specialties Negru, Codru, and Lidia. They are all extraordinary. Although I am not a connoisseur, I appreciate good wine, and I appreciate these, especially the Negru, with its rich dark red color and dry complexity redolent of berry, pepper, and, perhaps, even a little bit of the breath of God. Here in the cloistered, cool stillness of this cellar, after three or four glasses, any mysterious thing seems possible.

Other rooms house younger wines not ready for drinking. "They are sleeping gently just now," Stefan says tenderly as he runs a hand over the wood of a maturing Chardonnay. "We won't wake them.

Not yet." The wine from these cellars is never sold and is consumed primarily by the monks here. As far as I know, it is also never bottled.

The stairs seem steeper as we climb back into the late afternoon light an hour later. Across the yard, we return to Paisie's quarters, where we are ushered into his private dining room. Platityzn's limp is now more pronounced, but I do not know if it is from his exertions up the steep stairs or from the wine. Again we are greeted with the irrepressible laugh, dazzling smile, and playful eyes. Paisie insists I sit at his right and then pours each of us a glass of cabernet from a large clay pitcher. He squeezes my arm gently. "For an American, you're thin. That's good. A little late lunch won't hurt you."

As we eat this "little late lunch," the sun blasts through the large French windows bathing the small dining room in a shimmering, golden glow. The same unsmiling acolyte silently lays out the dishes on the linen-clad table: thinly sliced potatoes in sour cream and dill sauce; mackerel with garlic; coleslaw; chopped eggs with onions; huge black mushrooms sliced thinly, breaded and fried to a lovely light brown; sautéed trout with olive oil and lemon; wonderful fresh dark bread; and tomatoes and scallions with sharp feta.

Throughout the meal, Father Paisie continues to serve us wine as soon as our glasses approach empty. The talk is mostly of food, wine, and the ambitious building project just begun here, a new two-story dormitory to house many more students. The money for this comes largely from Church funds from Moscow and Bucharest. Platitzyn, apparently, has been helpful in ways the young prelate does not explain. "Let us simply say that both the Lord and Platitzyn work in mysterious ways," he says and laughs.

Platitzyn nods and empties his glass.

It sounds clichéd, but Paisie radiates joy and serenity. I feel it coming from him like heat from a hearth. He presides over this table like a proud father. I ask him if he is always this buoyant. He reflects for only an instant, then nods emphatically. "Yes, absolutely. Why shouldn't I be? I live in God's service." He takes a bite of trout. "My job is to live by example. In this region we have all kinds of people and my joy is God's joy. He doesn't distinguish between Romanians, Russians, Turks, Serbs, Greeks, Gagauz." He tugs at my sleeve and laughs. "Even Americans! It makes no difference to Him, and it makes no difference to me. The politics is for others."

Gazing out the window as we eat dessert—fresh strawberries dipped in beet sugar—he laughs again. "Our lives, all of this, are a gift. We need to understand this simple point. We need to know it. To really know it."

The sky is cloudless as we say our good-byes to Paisie and step back outside, where the flat, late afternoon light seems to make the blue-domed main cathedral across the small courtyard pulsate with an eerie, pinkish glow. Monks scurry past us as the bells atop the tower ring them back to prayer and the candle-cradled coolness of the domed sanctuary, the air heavy with the scent of apple blossoms and lilac.

One hour later, as promised in the first day's itinerary—"a meeting with the representative of a small and average business in Tiraspol"—Nicolae, Platitzyn, and I sit at a table in a cramped office across from Petyr Ivanovich Raiter. He has a pinched, sullen face with nervous eyes that will not look at me directly. He plays with a pencil, moving it through his fingers. Raiter, who is Ceban's son-in-law, makes irrigation pipe and culverts out of recycled plastic. Employing fifteen people, he rents production and office space from the government in a former furniture factory, which, like most of Tiraspol's state-owned industry, is largely idle. Lacking connections in the government, he has relied on seed money from family and friends to start this business. "The PMR is nothing," he says with a snort, "although I'm sure my friend Anatol Philipovich would disagree."

Platitzyn's eyes bore into him. His voice is edgy, hard. "No one can correctly say we are nothing. The PMR exists because it has been *forced* to exist."

Raiter shrugs. "You see? But I am also sure Anatol Philipovich will agree with what I say next, that we're not going anywhere with this idiotic regime. The pensioners listen to the propaganda and support this government, but real businessmen, the few of us who actually produce things, understand that things must somehow be changed. Of course, none of us has any idea how to do that. We are operating in a country that does not exist, a country that for the most part makes nothing but weapons, cognac, a little bit of steel, and a lot of crime."

Raiter, who is also Pentecostal, says his religious beliefs preclude political involvement: "I can only pray. But I am sure it is the best way. All is in God's hands. He works through us."

Raiter credits the power of prayer for the relative good fortune he has experienced in the past few years, a state of relative prosperity that contrasts starkly to the plight of most in both the PMR and Moldova proper. "I don't care what nonsense you hear from others, most of the people here suffer from this imposed isolation, stagnation, and a growing sense of hopelessness. What we have is only our faith. And because of that, because of the few of us who provide jobs, we are, ironically, keeping this terrible government alive. What changes we see will not come from them but from God. Only from God."

When we leave the idled furniture factory, Sasha drives through the center of town, which seems nearly deserted, continuing beyond the center. We drive to a late 1970s cluster of ten-story high-rises, indistinguishable from tens of thousands of others like them found anywhere in the former Soviet Union. Our apartment is large and furnished in typical *nomenklatura* Soviet style: ornate oriental carpets, wood floors, overstuffed living room furniture, and a hot water source independent of the municipal heating plant. It is on the outskirts of the city, in a narrow cul-de-sac. It is also unexpectedly luxurious.

Upstairs in our apartment, Platitzyn braces himself against the kitchen door. He points emphatically to his watch: "Eight thirty exactly. Sasha and I will be here with breakfast. For your own safety, I advise you not to leave the building tonight. You are not safe unescorted in this city."

*　　*　　*

At precisely eight thirty Monday morning, Platitzyn pounds on the apartment door. With brisk efficiency, he and Sasha unload four large bags of food onto the kitchen table: blini (Russian crepes), potato latkes with sour cream, garlic sausage, hot mustard, hard-boiled eggs, smoked sturgeon, and black bread. "Eat," Platitzyn growls. He removes his pressed suit jacket, drapes it over the back of a chair, and spears a sausage with a fork. "My wife made this."

Sasha joins us at the table, filling a plate with blini.

"They are already trying to kill us," Nicolae says, gesturing to the impressive array of food on the table. "It's an old Russian trick. Why use a gun when you can do the same thing with a fork?"

Platitzyn emits a staccato laugh: "You are calling my wife an assassin?"

Nicolae pops a piece of sturgeon into his mouth and shakes his head: "Not at all, Anatol Philipovich. I am calling her a virtuoso."

Regardless of the myth that vodka is scentless, there is the smell of it about our host this morning—one that grows stronger by late-morning after a visit to the editorial staff of *Dniesterovskaya Pravda*, founded in 1941. Officially published by the city government of Tiraspol, the eight-page tabloid is a mouthpiece for the Smirnov regime. The usual news features bland accounts of the president's meetings with dignitaries, who are generally conservative reactionary members of the Russian parliament. The editor, Tatyana Rudenko, assures us that the paper upholds "the highest standards of truthfulness and independence" by the editors and reporters, a spiel reminiscent of Svetlana Antonova's sermons to me at the Olvia-Press agency two years earlier.

Rudenko looks at me impassively across the narrow table. A mop of dyed red hair frames her rouged face. Behind large round glasses, ball-bearing eyes glance occasionally at a balding fat man in a greasy double-breasted suit. He remains silent throughout the entire interview. She smokes incessantly, tilting her head back with an odd theatrical flourish that accompanies each exhalation. I wait in vain for her to exhale through her nostrils.

Given his open disdain for the Smirnov regime, we are all aware that Platitzyn cannot publish in this, or any other paper, within the PMR. I ask about this, and the question is greeted by puzzled looks. "But Mr. Platitzyn has never submitted anything to us," Rudenko says, a suggestion of wounded innocence in her voice. "Of course, if he is a responsible journalist and does not slander the government there would be no problem."

When I ask how the paper is financed, Rudenko tells me, "Like any normal paper, we get our money from subscribers and advertisers." This is a strange assertion because there is zero advertising in the paper. "Excuse me, but, where are these advertisers?" I ask, pointing to the current issue.

Rudenko tells me she is uncomfortable with my questions. "This is not a proper question," she asserts. "You should act responsibly." Across the table, Platitzyn glowers. Nicolae has removed his glasses and begins rubbing the bridge of his nose.

I then ask if anyone has questions about the American media, any questions at all, noting that we have plenty of deficiencies and problems of our own. I assure them of my willingness to be completely honest. Finally, the bald man speaks: "Tell me please, how much does an American journalist make?"

As we leave the offices of the paper, which are in the city hall building, Platitzyn scowls and Nicolae fumes. When we pass yet another bust of Lenin out on the sidewalk, he asks Platitzyn why he wasted our time: "We sat for two hours having a group of criminally stupid people insult our intelligence! I remember some of these fossils from before," he says. "You knew what we would find here. Why did you do this?"

Platitzyn shrugs. "The meeting was for Mr. Shaw's benefit, not yours. He wants to see what is here, and I am showing him. That is what you want, isn't it?"

During a lunch across the broad Ulitsa 25 Oktober in the shaded courtyard of the Hotel Druzhba, our host consumes a carafe of vodka. He is well known to the waitresses, with whom he flirts aggressively. Towards the end of the meal, a striking, raven-haired young woman in a tight black miniskirt and a red acetate blouse stops by the table, the daughter of the restaurant manager. Platitzyn kisses her hand noisily. "Let me introduce Olga, this exquisite creature, to you," he says.

Olga rolls her eyes and laughs.

Platitzyn pours out four glasses of vodka: "A toast to the national pride of Mother Russia: our beautiful women!"

We toast to Olga, who now seems embarrassed.

Following this long (and, for Platitzyn, liquid) lunch, we are on our way to our meeting with the director of Moldovska School Number 20. Platitzyn launches into a very disjointed lecture about "theoretical" rights: "You will find this a good example of the kind of extensive rights this government guarantees the Romanian minority in the PMR. Pay close attention," he says. "I am sure this will prove interesting to you."

Set in a shady park, Moldovska School Number 20 is a flat, low-slung building that shares playground space with a regular Russian-language school. It is one of the few Romanian-language schools using the Latinate Romanian rather than the Soviet-era Cyrillic version that is still required elsewhere in the PMR. The existence of this school was a condition agreed upon as part of the ceasefire, ostensibly guaranteeing minority rights to the ethnic Romanians on the east bank of the river. Eight hundred twenty students attend this K-12 facility that is administered from Moldova proper.

The school's director is Ion Iovcev, a slightly stooped man with a soft voice and sad eyes underscored with dark pouches, testimonials to what he says is chronic exhaustion. His spare frame seems almost lost inside a baggy brown suit. He wears a rumpled white shirt with no tie. Platitzyn shakes his hand, introduces us, and turns to go. "I will wait in the car," he says and then lumbers down the long corridor towards the street.

"We are like hostages here," Iovcev tells us after closing the door. "We are always under observation. The KGB are often visiting us."

"And why is this?" I ask.

"Both I and my deputy director have been pressured to stop our activities here. They want us to leave Tiraspol and the PMR."

Those pressures, according to Iovcev, have taken many forms, all of them familiar to anyone who has lived in the Soviet Union. "I'm not talking about twenty years ago. I'm talking about last month, and last week. We are under constant assault here by these KGB thugs. There are the phone calls, sometimes twenty of them in an evening. In some cases, no one speaks on the other end and all you can hear is the sound of a person breathing. Always they speak in Russian."

Iovcev cradles the sides of his head in his hands, his elbows resting on the desk. "Other times, it is a specific threat or an obscenity, things out of a bad movie: 'Enjoy tomorrow, it will be your last day.' 'We know all about your life.' 'You are not safe.' 'Your throat will slice easily.' Things like that. Just stupid things. My wife and children have been threatened, too. This school has suffered a number of attacks on the building by unknown vandals; I do not understand how you can break windows and have no one hear the noise, but that is how it is around here.

"Once I was asked to come into police headquarters to discuss some problem with a vandalism attack on this building. A car came to get me, and then one of the men pressed a knife against my neck and suggested I consider a different occupation. I was terrified. I have never heard a colder voice."

I am appalled by what this man is telling me. I am also moved by his quiet, courageous defiance. Once again, Nicolae is rubbing the bridge of his nose, shaking his head slightly back and forth. I have heard no stories of Russians being treated this way in Chișinău, despite the official language policy. We are all quiet for what seems like a long time. "How can you keep doing this?" I ask finally.

Outside his window, children ride a line of swings, their shrieks of delight audible through the open window. Iovcev looks out at them and sighs. "I will *not* let them drive me out of here. I will fight for the interests of our children, in spite of the persecution. That is my reason to live."

As we leave his office, Iovcev warns us to be careful. "You will notice a black Lada parked across the intersection, just opposite us. Most likely you will notice two men inside. You can be sure they have noticed you."

Once out on the street, we spot the Lada as we return to the Mercedes to find Platitzyn passed out in the backseat, snoring loudly. Sasha paces the sidewalk in front of the Mercedes. "Anatol Philipovich is having a nap," he tells us, enunciating each word as if he is making a momentous pronouncement. "We'll come back in an hour," Nicolae tells him as we start to walk towards the center of town. A look of consternation crosses Sasha's face. "I am not supposed to leave you alone in the city."

"It's all right. We're just taking a walk," I say. "A simple walk in the afternoon sun. One hour. We are perfectly safe."

It has been only two days, but we are already beginning to feel like captives, constantly under the attentive eyes of our minder and his driver. We also wonder what he is trying to do and for whom he is doing it. We both wonder why he would facilitate a visit to Iovcev, for example. It makes no sense to either of us. We also do not understand his connections to the Pentecostals or to the monastery or why he was greeted with such warmth by Ceban and Father Paisie. Is he trying to establish the moral legitimacy of the PMR through what appears to be unfettered practice of religion? Is he trying to discredit the Smirnov regime by taking us to Iovcev?

"Who knows? I suspect he's working for Russia," Nicolae says, "but all he will tell you is he is retired from the Soviet military, nothing more. Of course, there is always more."

Even at five o'clock on a fine afternoon in early May, downtown Tiraspol is nearly lifeless. With a little paint and reparation, the city would be attractive with its graceful Corinthian-pilastered buildings in the Russian provincial style lining the wide main street, but most of those are a faded gray-brown with peeling façades. Mostly, Tiraspol remains drab and neglected, a city seemingly without a civic pulse, every bit the ghost town we felt it to be two years earlier.

Unlike Chișinău, the sidewalks here are devoid of pedestrians, and traffic is thin on the main drag, Ulitsa 25 Oktober, which makes it easy to spot the black Lada driving towards us from the opposite direction. Nicolae points to the little sedan: "This is perfect, another artifact. This is killing me!" he groans. "Time travel *is* possible, we've just proven it, right back to the Soviet Union. Fuck them. I am getting a headache."

A horn blasts, and I turn to see the orange Mercedes, which pulls up beside us. Platitzyn is now back in the front seat, apparently refreshed from his nap. Scowling, he climbs out and we continue walking, the Mercedes idling by the curb.

Platitzyn nods towards the street: "Did you notice we are being followed?

The black Lada is now parked across the boulevard. Two men stand outside the car smoking.

"Yes, we saw them. Someone should teach them to be less obvious," I say.

Platitzyn wags a finger at me. "It seems you do not understand the subtleties of the craft. Someone doesn't want them to be less obvious. Believe me, they are capable of great subtlety. Artistically so. No, they are simply and efficiently sending a message. And that is why I *must* insist you do not walk around here without protection."

The Lada now pulls away from the curb and the three of us watch it drive out of sight. Platitzyn jabs a finger into my chest. "You are *my* responsibility, and I take my responsibilities seriously," he says. "I intend to keep you safe. Let me tell you a story about a group of German businessmen I was assisting here about a month ago. One of them stupidly photographed a bridge just on the edge of the city. He was actually photographing a slogan painted on the bridge—'In Unity We Are Strong!'—but he was arrested on espionage charges. You must remember that this remains an extremely sensitive military area, and people are nervous."

"What happened to the Germans?" I ask.

"It was resolved, but it was expensive for them. If people want something to happen to you here, and you do not have protection, it will. They could make you disappear without anyone being able to prove you ever crossed the border."

We are now standing by a giant statue of Alexander Suvorov, Russia's greatest military genius, the founder of Tiraspol, scourge of the Turks, Poles, Italians, and Napoleon. It dominates the large park across from the War Memorial. Little known in the West, Suvorov is credited with being the major factor in expanding Catherine the Great's imperial ambitions that enabled the Kremlin to extend its reach from Europe to the Far East. Suvorov waves a saber atop a rearing stallion, frozen in heroic exhortation.

Platitzyn points to the statue. "Every Soviet officer had to study this man's life. He clarified the nature of military action for all the world, a far greater general than Napoleon, maybe even greater than Alexander the Great," he said. "The essence was speed, force, and flexibility. And always at the service of diplomacy. We should have remembered that."

The great general's image appears on every PMR banknote, and I wonder how he would feel knowing that he graces a currency regarded as a bad joke by those forced to use it.

Back in the Mercedes, we stop for coffee at Terasa Capital, a small outdoor café beneath a large green canopy sporting Coke and Sprite logos. Sasha has insisted on this place. Grinning, he points upward to the peaked tent ceiling: "This is very nice, very modern," he says. "Very sophisticated. I love this place!" It is, in fact, extremely pleasant sitting here overlooking Ulitsa 25 Oktober in the early evening. Nicolae, Sasha, and I order Baltika beer, while Platitzyn orders a carafe of vodka and a bowl of peanuts. A young man dressed in black trousers, black turtleneck, and a sports jacket approaches our table and greets Platitzyn, who then introduces us. Oleg Serov is a reporter for the government-controlled TV station in Tiraspol. He is on the way to an interview, he tells us, but he stays long enough for me to invite him to meet back at the apartment later in the evening. After the young man walks away, Platitzyn shakes his head: "Why do you want to talk to him? I'm telling you right now: you will gain nothing. He has a good heart but a weak mind."

I nod: "I am sure I will learn something from him, maybe as much as what I gained from our meeting this morning with *Dniesterovskaya Pravda*. In any event, it is another voice," I say, feeling annoyed by my host's officiousness. He cannot understand that I really *do* want to hear as many voices as I can during this short trip. He cannot understand that I find this all impenetrable.

While the iron fist remains visible here, even more important ultimately is the Soviet-style media's role in creating and sustaining public support for both the Smirnov government and for the deepening separation between the PMR—now eight years into independence—and Moldova proper. Platitzyn is quick to point out that according to numerous polls, 80 percent of the region's 650,000 inhabitants support continued independence and closer ties to Russia. But to his dismay, the Smirnov regime itself also still commands support from key sectors of the PMR population, particularly pensioners, who tend to be conservative and have traditionally opposed market reforms, and also from the young.

Oleg Serov is one of those who have helped maintain that support. He is also at this moment somewhat nervous, here in the kitchen of our rented flat, facing an increasingly inebriated and truculent Platitzyn, who is leaning against the counter with a new bottle of vodka. Our minder's suit jacket is tossed carelessly on the living room couch, and he has removed his tie and rolled up his shirtsleeves. Sasha has retreated to the living room to watch an installment of *Santa Barbara* broadcast from Moscow. Platitzyn scowls at our guest. "Why are you here?" he barks. "For whom, exactly, do you work?"

Nicolae stands at the doorway and puts two fingers to his neck, the classic Russian gesture for drunkenness. I remind him gently that we invited Oleg after meeting him at Terasa Capital. Watching him glower at this twenty-three-year old man, I have no trouble imagining him conducting an interrogation in his military intelligence days. What I imagine disturbs me.

I have noticed that the more he drinks, the sadder he becomes and the closer to the surface is his loathing for Smirnov.

Although we have not spoken of this in depth, his role as advisor to General Lebed, and by association his support for the founding regime of the PMR, must be painfully problematic for him.

Finally, Nicolae manages to coax Platitzyn out of the kitchen, but as he lumbers out he continues to glare at Oleg. I have seen this specific glare many times in this part of the world, and as he leaves I wonder if it is part of a standard KGB training course: Lethal Looks 101.

Within minutes, Platitzyn is "resting his eyes" on the couch, and Oleg is able to relax as we sip strong, sweet coffee in red enameled espresso cups and nibble on bitter Russian chocolate. We are talking about journalists and their responsibilities. I tell him I am genuinely curious about his perspective and about how he views his profession. "Like journalists anywhere, my job," he tells me, "is to tell the truth to the people and help social improvement."

Sasha keeps returning to the kitchen, for water, for bread, but he remains close by the door when he leaves.

I like Oleg. He is soft spoken and open, and with his neatly combed brown hair and clean-shaven face, he seems decent and honest. He also seems to have the ability to simultaneously entertain two diametrically opposed notions. "I must reflect the state ideology, to mold social opinion and to stress the need for our continued orientation to Moscow and the former Soviet states," he tells me.

At the same time, he insists the press is free here, and when I ask about the absence of any opposition media, he shrugs. "That's an economic matter, not a political one," he says. "We had an opposition paper, but it closed because of financial reasons. Being a state media, our costs are covered by the government, so if you work outside the system, you have to find the money somewhere else."

However, working "outside the system" can be problematic. One opposition publication had been run out of the PMR, primarily through regular confiscation of all its editions on newsstands and by attacks on individual journalists. Another only mildly critical of the Smirnov regime was harassed out of existence by lawsuits that were upheld by the puppet Supreme Court.

These examples seem to make him as uncomfortable as the colonel's glare. "Well, maybe there's more to these stories than we know," he tells me.

And if he writes a story critical of the system? "Well, I am not critical of this government," he answers.

"But if you *were* and you *did* write something embarrassing, what would happen to you?"

"If I did that, I would not have a job, obviously," he says. "There are certain controls. As in any normal place. But I am not controlled. I report the truth as I see it."

He is most proud, he says, of being part of a media that has deeply shaped the opinions of a new generation coming of age in the PMR. "Our future is with Russia or some kind of new Soviet Union, not with the West," he says. "That's my job, to make them understand."

Later, as Oleg leaves, Platitzyn regards the young man stonily, jabbing his index finger at him. "You need to be careful how you choose your friends, young man," he says. "Believe me, I know. Serving the state and serving the government are not the same thing." The door closes behind him, and I hear his retreating footsteps echoing on the concrete stairs. Platitzyn turns to me: "Don't waste your time writing about him. Only a fool or a thief could work for this government, and I don't think he's a thief."

By Tuesday, things are deteriorating as Platitzyn begins drinking earlier and earlier. How he has the time or the stamina, I do not know. We have spent the morning in a tidy village just outside of the city, a village that is ostensibly "typical." In one respect it is: brightly colored stucco houses with asbestos-tiled hip roofs flank the tree-lined streets. They are tucked behind gates back from the rutted road. But this village is mostly Pentecostal, and therefore perhaps a bit more prosperous than others, Platitzyn tells us before Sasha stops in front of a green metal gate. Inside is a small compound with a blue stucco main house and a few tiny outbuildings for animals. A large garden stretches behind the house. We are here, at the Danilov residence, and Platitzyn has gone inside after being welcomed like a brother; Nicolae has collapsed in a hammock in the shade, just against the outside wall of the house, suddenly stricken with a migraine. "Oh my God," he moans, "I cannot stand any more of this. Please, just let me stay out here. If I'm lucky, I will die."

I soon find myself in a living room sitting across from Alexandria, a severe, slightly cross-eyed seven-year-old girl in a plain blue dress who is playing an accordion with great concentration and very little skill. I smile encouragingly, muttering the few nice words in Russian that I can muster while her mother Anna, a small woman with plaited dark hair, beams proudly.

Through the doorway I see Platitzyn and Danilov talking intensely. A minute later, Platitzyn drops to his knees, clasps his hand in a gesture of prayer and begins to babble incomprehensibly. He spews forth a torrent of what I suppose are words, but I have never heard anything remotely like it. At first I think he must be experiencing a seizure, but I then realize what I am witnessing: the man is speaking in tongues, lost in the Holy Spirit. This lasts only about half a minute—long enough, however, for me to understand perhaps a little more about him. While Pentecostals do not uniformly shun liquor, its consumption to excess is widely regarded as sinful. Poor Platitzyn.

*   *   *

It is now almost evening, and we are back at the apartment. Across the street, an old man grazes nine scrawny goats in a field dotted with small gardens. Huge concrete high-tension pylons loom behind him, and beneath them the remains of unfinished apartment blocks decay in the lowering sun. In the courtyard directly beneath the living room window, an old woman cleans a rug that is hanging from a steel support by whacking it repeatedly with a wide plank. The dust flies, and each blow sounds like a gunshot as it echoes off the peeling cement façades of the surrounding buildings. Platitzyn and I are discussing modern European history, especially Soviet history. He tells me he is a native of the Donbas region of eastern Ukraine and can remember the German army occupying his village and then troops billeting in his family's house during World War II. In what he considers "an interesting turn of events," he later served for many years as part of the Soviet occupying forces in East Germany. Working as a high-level translator and an intelligence analyst in the GRU, he also served for eight years as part of the Soviet delegation overseeing the imprisonment of Rudolf Hess in Spandau Prison. But today he does not want to talk about Germany, a country he says he greatly admires for its discipline, culture, and intellect.

Today we are talking about the demise of the Soviet Union. Actually, we are arguing. Platitzyn shakes his head and smiles grimly as he pours another round of Kvint cognac. "No, you have it wrong, my American friend. It wasn't suicide," he says. "It was murder. Fratricide, the worst kind."

Like more than ten thousand other Soviet army personnel, Platitzyn retired to Transnistria, to what would become the PMR. Compared to many places in the former Soviet Union, it is an ideal place to retire. It has an agreeable climate, ample housing, a large veterans' hospital, and on the old Soviet pensions, four times what he now receives, one could live well here where the wine is both cheap and excellent.

It should have been a happy retirement, but as with millions of other former Soviet citizens, the last decade has been a disaster for him. "None of this should have happened. It was never a reflection of the majority of people within the Soviet Union, and certainly not the majority here in Transnistria," he asserts as he pours another round and begins to lay out his version of recent Soviet history. "The leaders of Russia, Ukraine, and Belarus had a secret meeting, and with the idea that each of them would become the power in their region, they decided to split up the Soviet Union: The Baltic republics got their independence, which was right because they had been unlawfully occupied and annexed by the USSR. But those Slavic leaders betrayed all the Caucasus and the middle Asian republics. They lied to everybody. Under a new union treaty proposal by Gorbachev, we were told the borders would be open, no customs, no controls. We were told the army and defense forces would be united. Again, a big lie.

"If they had told the people the army would be dismembered, that the weapons would become the tools of criminals, that the borders would become mined, that each region would have its own worthless currency, and the majority would see a sharp drop in their living standards and life expectancy, millions of people would have taken to the streets to protest this travesty. And you must understand, what we have now is a disaster, a tragedy. Tens of millions have been plunged back into the darkness, into misery, starvation, and premature deaths. We have a very dangerous, unstable, chaotic situation."

He has a point. Statistics released annually by the United Nations Development Program paint a nasty picture of life in many of the former Soviet republics. Excepting Latvia, Lithuania and Estonia, life expectancy, even in Russia, has declined precipitously while infant mortality rates have climbed; public health and education systems are close to collapse; wages for the majority have plummeted along with pensions for the retired; and prices for basic survival staples have soared, as has the power of organized crime. New governments remain to varying degrees autocratic, and human rights violations continue to be widespread, especially for journalists and opposition leaders. Also troubling is another toxic legacy of the

Soviet Union—pervasive environmental pollution and little money to deal with it.

Platitzyn directs part of his scorn at the West. "Western notions of democracy have been part of the problem," he insists. "When people are poor, materially and spiritually, they cannot be given political freedom. This kind of democracy changes its meaning and becomes something else. It turns into a situation where anything is allowed and everyone acts for himself only, never for the good of the country. In these new times, if you steal a bicycle, you will go to jail, but if you steal the bicycle factory, you will keep it and get rich."

Nor does Platitzyn spare any wrath for the current Tiraspol regime. "During that stupid war in 1992, there was only one real motivation on both sides: the greed of the leaders for power and money. Smirnov must go," he insists, his tone sharp and bitter. "You have seen this for yourself already. His people are a bunch of crooks, gangsters, and traitors to the people who have supported them. We had a legitimate case for self-determination, but there is no legitimacy for this government."

Although contemptuous of Smirnov, Platitzyn, like most ethnic Slavs living in the PMR, blames the secession problem primarily on the former leaders in Chişinău. These men, he says, recast the independence question as an ethnic one and by so doing set irrevocable events in motion.

"Ten years ago the leaders in Chişinău declared Moldova to be brothers with the Romanian people and they wanted to join them. Well, what about the forty percent of us who are Slavs?" Platitzyn chops the air with his hand, his voice growing louder, harder. "Now they don't proclaim this openly anymore, and they have nothing to sell their own people who now leave by the tens of thousands to find work because in Moldova they have no chance. They had a saying: 'The Russians over the Dniester, the Jews in it.' Well, their misery is God's punishment for what they tried to do. *They* forced this situation, not us, but the results are tragic for both sides."

I ask him if, knowing what he does now, he still would have supported Lebed's intervention on the behalf of the separatists and the creation of this breakaway republic. He grows quiet and regards me with a look I cannot read. There is a long silence, punctuated only by the kids kicking a soccer ball below the window. He glances over at the window, then back to me. "That might be an easy question for you to ask, but it is not one that is easy for me to answer. If I live long enough, maybe I will know. That is all I can say."

"So, what *really* needs to happen to end this mess?" I ask. "Annexation of the PMR to Russia? The return of some kind of Soviet Union?"

Platitzyn fills our glasses again. He gives me another long look and then simply shrugs. "Not the way you mean. Look, if you think I'm simply an ardent admirer of the old Soviet system, you're very wrong. Twenty-two years ago, I voluntarily returned my Communist Party card because my conscience would not put up with the gap between the propaganda and what I saw in real life.

"At the time what I did was considered professional suicide because I might have had a much better career, and today you and I might have met on a very different level, if we met at all. But there are principles in life. All of that ideology was based on lies."

He gets up from the couch with a grunt and walks slowly to the window. At this moment there is no hardness about him, nothing of the aggressive man used to being in command. If anything, he looks deflated, haunted. He sighs. "You've seen something of this place and of Moldova. These aren't countries. These are amputated limbs. Thirty-five years ago I took a pledge to the Soviet people when I joined the army. Now I am free of that oath," he says bitterly. "There is no Soviet people, no Soviet army, no Soviet Union, no Soviet state. There is only my heart, and in there I remain loyal to that oath."

He looks at me, his eyes almost beseeching: "Can you understand any of this? Anything at all?"

*   *   *

Platitzyn's promises of a meeting with journalism faculty and students at Tiraspol State University have unraveled. It would have been an interesting conversation, but apparently such a meeting is "administratively impossible" at this time. "It doesn't matter," Nicolae says. "Just give us a ride to the university. We'll find something."

Platitzyn does not like this suggestion. "They will not let you on the grounds," he insists. "If you go in, there will be trouble, and I will not be able to help you."

Nicolae shrugs. "Then we'll simply stand outside and talk with students there."

In a tree-lined park in the center of Tiraspol, Galya, a third-year linguistics student in a short skirt and blouse, gestures contemptuously towards the university just behind her. She flicks her bottle-blonde hair away from her face. "All the real professors have left," she tells Nicolae and me. "Our degrees will be worthless anywhere else because the university has lost its accreditation. Now all we have is a banana university in a banana republic. This place is a bad joke. Smirnov is shitting on all of us, and we have to buy the toilet paper. Everything he does is to take care of his family, and there's nothing left for us."

For Aleksei, a denim-clad classmate of Galya, the lack of hope is bad enough. Worse still is the oppressive sense of isolation. "We live in a state that doesn't exist. How can that be? It's a country with no law," he says between nervous drags of a cigarette. "Here you can't rely on the government, on the cops, on anybody but maybe your family. We are alone in this republic. To the world, we don't exist. If we could only become part of Russia, then things would be much better for us. Putin must help us. We can't do anything ourselves."

Nicolae listens glumly to the students, and as they walk away he says, "Just look around you. This is a very metaphysically interesting place. It defies the laws of time. There is no future here, only this grotesque present. Watch what happens where nobody wants to commit to a path. Instead, on both sides of this river we're waiting for something else to happen—from Putin, from America, from Europe, from God himself. This is a demented farce. We lost the USSR; then we lost our brothers. We haven't a past, we haven't a future. I want to scream."

Platitzyn sits stiffly in the front seat of the Mercedes, staring out at the students who pass him by. More than generations separate them. The gulf is immense and beyond bridging. I too want to scream. Nobody I have met on this trip has escaped the fallout of recent history, of the Soviet collapse, of this civil war in a corner of the world few Americans have even heard of. There is a sad ugliness, a deep melancholia of the spirit that hangs over much of this place, and to a lesser extent in Moldova too. At this moment I feel the weight, however ephemerally, of this sadness. I know that tens of millions of former Soviet citizens remain bound to a common and convoluted web of myth and mystery. I know this in the abstract. But Nicolae Pojoga, Anatol Philipovich Platitzyn, Ghennady and Natalia Sokolov, Ion Iovcev, Petyr Raiter, Oleg Serov, and these university students are not simple abstractions; they are people living difficult and troubled lives, exiled by circumstance, stumbling from the wreckage of a ruined empire into a present they could never have imagined.

GLEBUS

Chișinău, November 2004

From the outside, this building away from the city center appears to be just another dingy Khrushchev-era apartment block, set off from the main road, shaded by oaks and beech. Only upon closer inspection do I realize that the north face of the compound is mostly glass and that I am looking at the outside of maybe forty artists' studios, a leftover perk from the Soviet era when at least some artists were subsidized.

For nearly half a century, Moldova's greatest living painter, Glebus Sainciuc, has worked in number twenty six. I am inside his studio, and I am being watched. Hundreds of faces peer out from the walls, crowding together, up and over a doorway, up a balcony wall, perched on the railing sixteen feet above the floor. Some of these people are familiar to me: Solzhenitsyn, looking characteristically lugubrious, eyebrows arched in a disconcerting frown, peers out from above the doorway; composer Eugen Doga leers like a sybarite, a shock of curly hair ringing his magnificent bald pate; Luciano Pavarotti is there, ready to break into an aria; peering through his trademark heavy round spectacles, lips pursed, Jean-Paul Sartre gazes pensively across the large room while his fellow countryman Marcel Marceau, ever silent, watches it all in mild amusement. I don't recognize many of the faces, but they are all very much present, replete with verisimilar smiles, frowns, and grimaces. Some are frozen in mid-laugh, mid-yawn, or mid-shout. The eyes are uncannily animated, which, of course, accounts for my unnerving feeling of being watched. Some of those eyes seem to follow me as I walk across the room.

Glebus has been dabbling in life masks for fifty years, amassing a long list of clients along the way. He stands before me now in a doorway, showing them off, playing the entertainer. He is clad in a tacky purple robe, grasping a fake microphone made of a ball of aluminum foil and a short wooden stick. On his head is a mask of Alla Pugacheva, a famous Russian pop star, and he takes a deep coquettish bow, mimicking her trademark concert finish. Muffled laughter seeps out from behind the mask.

The short, compact man then darts behind the curtain and returns holding two perfectly accurate renditions of his own face, one in his right hand, one in his left. He peers out between them. The center face is grinning while the mouths of the other two are poised between perplexity and seriousness. But all three have the same remarkably clear blue eyes. They are the vivid, intelligent eyes of an observer who misses nothing. There is something else too, a flash of mischief, maybe even a touch of anarchy. Poised between wonder and a giggle, they have the look of someone who finds life amusing. These are not the eyes of an eighty-four-year-old man.

A brittle light penetrates the wall of dirty, streaked glass to the center of this cavernous room, illuminating the weathered face of Moldova's preeminent painter. Compact and wiry, he gives the impression of motion even while standing still, as if his thin layer of skin can barely contain the energy beneath. He is dressed in brown canvas pants, an oversized black denim jacket, under which is a heavy wool sweater, and a tattered blue-and-green plaid flannel shirt with a frayed collar.

Another wall is covered with paintings, many of them his, others by his wife and son. Most are portraits, including a magnificent self-portrait done in 1994 that would not be out of place in a Renoir exhibit. Four battered and very old straight-backed chairs line the bottom part of this wall, around which runs a shelf propping up dozens of small prints, tubes of acrylic and oil paint, a pile of rags, and a violin with one string. Across the room, an unfinished portrait of a girl with long red hair sits on a large easel. The floor is covered with the ubiquitous worn gray linoleum common to so many Soviet flats.

Nicolae has often spoken of Glebus, who has been a friend and mentor of sorts to him for most of his adult life, and I am delighted to be received with such warmth.

"We'll make a deal," he says. "You want to interview me; that's fine, but I will draw you at the same time. And we have to start, while the light is still good."

He points to an unlit bank of fluorescent lights hanging from the ceiling. "Please excuse the cold, but there is no electricity or gas for heat for the moment because I am having a dispute with the city," he explains. "It's not an interesting dispute, very ordinary, embarrassingly so, I'm afraid: they want more money and I can't pay it."

It is odd but pleasant, sitting close enough so that our knees nearly touch, one of the twentieth century's great artists peering over a large sketchpad, his eyes fixed on my face. I realize we are both trying to do the same thing—illuminate a person, I with words, he with an image. "You look like a diplomat, maybe from the UN," he says teasingly as his hand moves constantly over the paper. "Of course you'd be a terrible diplomat."

"And why would I be a terrible diplomat?" I ask. "Have I just been insulted?"

Glebus laughs. "Not at all. I only mean that your face is transparent, like the windows facing you. You would not be a good professional liar. Believe me, I know. I've painted enough of them."

The right hand is moving steadily, its progress mysterious on the other side of the pad as he sketches. "Sometimes I can capture about ten percent of a person in a quick sketch: maybe thirty percent in a good drawing, and sometimes more in a real portrait. For me, this is detective work and I must find clues. For a portrait to succeed for me, I have to capture the soul, the essence of a person. It's the same thing with all the masks. Sometimes it's easy, like with you. Other times, it can be very hard, especially if a person is closed and tight within himself."

As we talk and he studies me, I study him, wanting to render a perfect likeness of this wonderful, animated face that watches me so intently. His high, creased forehead is crowned with a thatch of thinning gray hair that sticks straight up on the top, giving him the look of someone who has just stepped in from the wind. The weathered skin is spotted and nearly translucent, as it is with many old people, and a prominent blood vessel snakes down each side of his forehead to the temples. Others spread out along his bulbous nose, beneath which is a trimmed white moustache that cloaks a mobile, thin-lipped mouth. His ears are disproportionately long and they protrude. The effect is at once comic and boyish, but prominent cheekbones work against that impression, lending an almost gaunt quality to his face. Bushy eyebrows sit on a slightly protruding brow—a face of angles and intersections. Deeply etched lines fan out across his cheeks, and around his eyes, especially when he smiles, which today, anyway, seems to be frequently. But most of all it is the eyes that hold my attention. They would be less surprising on a mischievous, precocious child.

His right hand continues to work quickly. "I am a soul hunter, a kind of Sherlock Holmes looking for clues," he says. "But instead of poking into cellars and drawers, I look for them in the face, in the body, the voice. I have to paint from the inside out."

When I ask him about his years under the Soviets, he pauses for a moment, and then he laughs. "Here is where you want me to tell you something extravagant, something dramatic, but I can't tell you *anything* heroic. It was just that the Communists didn't know what to do with me for a long time. They wanted me to just do propaganda. I was hired to paint official portraits, but I couldn't always do what they wanted."

"What did they want?"

"Something serious, something full of pompous dignity," he continues with a derisive snort. "I'm not interested in pompous dignity. I have no appreciation for it. Except maybe for a cartoon."

The arm stops periodically, shifting, adding, and erasing, the blue eyes probing my face. I am fully clothed, marginally insulated against the cold, but I feel oddly naked at the same time. Behind us the north light is beginning to grow just a little bit dimmer.

"I refused to join the Party but I did become a member of the Union of Artists, and that gave me at least a little legitimacy." Glebus looks up from the pad, fixes his eyes on me briefly, and then returns to the page with a sigh. "They wanted stern, mythical paintings. Every politician a hero, but I just couldn't do it. Many times I saw a child uncomfortable in his adult clothing, and somewhere in the painting, I always found a place to make a little joke, or I found the kid inside, the uncorrupted man. So, many of my portraits, *especially* the ones of Lenin, were rejected."

He looks up briefly, his eyes once again probing.

I ask if this was a difficult time for him, and he emphatically shakes his head.

"No," he says. "Why should it have been? I had my family, my art, and in a very strange way, my freedom. I was of little importance to them, so no one bothered with me. But I made a living, with my masks, some official portraits, some art lessons, and a little architectural work. You won't find a story here full of pain and suffering with me."

Glebus tells me he eventually found himself in better circumstances after his masterpiece, *Masa Mare*, won a series of awards at several Moscow exhibitions in 1960. It is a magnificent impressionist depiction of a country wedding, a far cry from the rote Soviet-realism style promoted by Khrushchev, who railed against the Soviet modernist painters. The Union of Artists proclaimed it a masterpiece, and he found himself in the unaccustomed position of enjoying a degree of official favor. "It was very odd, but after that, I was given my own studio—this one—and told to paint whatever I wanted. Simply incredible."

Glebus stops for a moment and then chuckles. "And they, at least, paid for my heat and lights. That one picture opened the world to me and I then became known in the West. It was good propaganda for Moscow, even if they were too stupid to understand at first!"

He makes one more adjustment and then turns the pad around. I am now staring at a caricature of myself, a very accurate one. He smiles, deep laugh lines radiating from the corners of his eyes, the nose crinkling. "It's all a matter of focus, you see." He leans over and points to my eyes. "For your face, that was the key—that and your big nose of course."

Glebus scampers up the ship's ladder to the balcony, the staccato slap of his shoes against the treads echoing off the cement walls. "I have to show you something before the light fades any more," he shouts down at me. He returns a few minutes later with a large roll, maybe four feet long, tucked under one arm. Squatting down on his haunches, he unrolls it, spreading it out to a length of about twenty feet.

I stare down in amazement at dozens of sketches glued to a faux-wood-grained plastic roll: they are all signed by the various sketchers. And they are all of cows. Many are crudely drawn stick-figure renditions, really, while others are executed with great artistry.

"*This*," Glebus says, "is my unique collection, my obsession. Just look at this! Imagine. Here is Julio Iglesias' cow. There it is!" he says, squatting down again and pointing to a whimsical creature looking very much like Ferdinand the Bull. And Sartre's cow, a most thoughtful animal." He points to a poorly drawn sausage-like creature with a pensive cast to the mouth and a very prominent udder: "You see, beyond all that philosophy, look at that udder: he was a typical Frenchman after all!

"And here is Pavarotti's cow. Very fat, as you see. Even Solzhenitsyn couldn't get out of this." He jabs a finger at a rather pathetic-looking creature. "A most serious, skinny, and dignified cow from a great Russian soul."

Spread out before me are cows drawn by ambassadors, actors, poets, singers, journalists, politicians, and everyday people. "Usually I require that my visitors draw a cow for me, before I paint them or mask them. It breaks down the formality," he explains.

"But why cows?" I ask. It is getting colder in the studio with the fading light, but he doesn't seem to notice.

"When I was eight years old, I had an art class and we were all asked by the teacher to draw a cow," he replies. "When I showed the class mine, everyone laughed at me. The teacher was annoyed. 'Stop it,' she said. 'This happens to be good. It's a very nice cow, and it also happens to be unique, like all of your cows. Glebus is the *only* person in the world who could have drawn his cow. I could never draw the same thing.' I owe her my life, that wonderful woman. She encouraged me to continue, and suddenly I felt I had respect. I think when people draw a cow, they become eight years old, and then I can feel them. Believe me, it humbles the mighty."

Unlike most Moldovans I have met, Glebus seems truly happy, immune to the ramifications of post-Soviet life and its attendant anxieties. He seems to have neither the Russian proclivity for brooding nor the Romanian one for melodrama. He seems, at least on first impression, to be deeply in love with living.

When I note this, he stops drawing for a moment, purses his lips, and nods. At this moment, only the eyes smile. "I have been accused of this before," he says, "often by my own friends, but I have never seen the point in worrying. If it is beyond my control, what on earth is the point? I see no value in being a victim, of suffering or of being a tormented artist. I leave that to others. As Voltaire said, 'I have made a choice to be happy.'"

Given this land's troubled history, I wonder how difficult that choice must have been at times, but he dismisses my speculation with an impatient flick of the hand. Such thoughts, apparently, have no place in this sanctuary.

As Glebus rolls up the sheet, he continues talking, his voice punctuated by a burping laugh that often erupts unexpectedly. "But these are not my favorite cows. The real masterpieces are in another of my collections." He rifles through a tall, battered bookcase full of boxes of brushes, tubes of paint, assorted sketchpads, and tins of turpentine, finally settling on a black and battered cardboard portfolio. Delicately he unties the bow that holds it closed and pulls out a large watercolor of three cows grazing in a pasture. It is clearly a young child's work. A golden sun with two eyes and a smile sits in the middle of a washed-out blue sky, just above the cows. Little bubbles of dialogue float above each bovine head. Glebus puts his cheek next to the drawing, smiling. "Isn't this amazing? It's brilliant. I give every child who draws a cow for me an official Baccalaureate of Cow certificate. Art is our natural language, so of course we all can do it."

The box is full of cow pictures, all done by young children, all of them Glebus's favorites. "How can I possibly have a favorite?" he asks me. "Each one of these is a miracle."

*   *   *

The National Opera House in Chişinău was built during a frenzy of new modernist construction in Moldova towards the end of the Breshnev era in 1980. It is from the outside a graceless, flat-roofed structure that squats heavily in the middle of a park-like expanse of lawn, connected to the broad Stefan cel Mare Boulevard by a long, imposing stairway. Inside, however, it is a pleasing mix of glass, stone, and wood. The auditorium itself is well engineered, sloping gently towards the large proscenium, and the acoustics are excellent.

Every Sunday this auditorium is invaded by hundreds of children from all over Moldova. This usually dignified home to one of the largest opera companies in Eastern Europe sounds more like a school gymnasium for a few hours, and kids, as Glebus says, "call the shots." They come, thanks largely to his successful petition to the Chişinău municipal government for a regular children's day in the capital.

The shows typically consist of a variety of vocal and dance acts by schoolchildren from villages and towns throughout the country: Călăraşi, Lăpusna, Rašćani, and Bălţi are represented today. What is remarkable, aside from this event taking place at all, is the care that is put into production. Sound and lighting are absolutely professional, as is the elegantly clad MC.

Glebus and I sit about twenty rows back from the stage. The four-hour show is now over, and the quality, apparently as always, has been uneven. A few acts were dazzling, like the modern jazz dancers from a high school in Bălţi and a crew of elementary school girls doing a scene from Swan Lake. Everyone has had equal time, and at these events, everyone is a winner. Kids now crowd around us, waiting for Glebus to work his sketch magic. One by one boys and girls kneel in the chair in front of him, facing backwards. "*You were incredible!*" Glebus says to a little ballerina, maybe five years old, sitting stiffly in front of him. Her long dark hair is elaborately braided into two pigtails, which trail down her shoulders. She still wears the little tiara on top of her head, and bits of glitter dot her cheeks. "Amazing! Magnificent! Brilliant!" Glebus cries. The little girl in the red tutu giggles self-consciously as he captures her joy in a few deft strokes.

"What's your name, Madame?" he asks with mock gravity.

"Doina," she replies, still giggling.

"Of course. Doina—a beautiful song. That's what you are, a beautiful song."

He scribbles a few lines in the bottom corner of the drawing, gently removes the sheet from the pad and hands it to her. The little girl's face brightens into a lovely smile as she stares at. She then clutches the paper to her chest and runs up the aisle.

From the stage a large perspiring woman in a blue skirt and sweater attempts to gather her class, several of whom have scattered throughout the performance hall. What decorum there had been is gone. Kids chase each other up and down the aisles, over the rows of seats, and back up onto the stage. The woman purses her lips, glares fiercely, stamps her foot, and points angrily to a mop-headed young boy. "Vioriel!" she shrieks. "Get up here now!"

Today I think Glebus seems much more like Peter Pan than Sherlock Holmes, and as we make our way down the long steps leading to the street, I tell him so. He laughs. "On days like this, maybe seventy-five or eighty years drop from me. It's a magical exchange of energy. Did you see them all on stage? Mistakes everywhere! Chaos! And who cares? Only the adults. It's wonderful how kids are masters of improvisation, especially when they're not supposed to be."

"Like you and the Soviet portrait commissions?" I ask.

Glebus grabs my arm, stopping mid-stride. He nods his head vigorously: "Exactly! That is *exactly* right. They can't help it any more than I could. That is why what kids do is so beautiful. They are little subversives, just like me! Days like this prove what I have always known: every child can discover his own genius, and our job—yours and mine—is to help them find it. Maybe our most important job."

For a short man, Glebus walks amazingly fast. It's as if his shoes are somehow spring-loaded. He leans into his strides, shoulders hunched, head thrust forward like a human battering ram, and I have to work to keep up with him. Half the city seems to be out walking on this sun-dappled November afternoon, as is the custom here: the last of the golden leaves cling tenaciously to the large old oaks that line the sidewalks, the bright, flat afternoon light accenting the gold. Despite the forty-degree chill, Chişinău seems to glow. Husbands and wives, many dressed elegantly in their one good suit or dress, babies in arms or in strollers, older ones hanging on to hands and wrists, crowd the park across from the opera house. At an elaborate belle-époque water fountain, parents pay a few lei for their children to drive small red, green, orange, and yellow battery-powered cars, their little faces intently concentrating as they steer in languid circles. The smell of roasting peanuts and popcorn from nearby vendors fills the air, mixing with the poignant perfume of dried, fallen leaves.

He continues to talk as we pass these children, gesturing dramatically with a sweep of his right arm: "My sweet, beautiful city," he says smiling. "After all of the madness and idiocy, we have kept our glorious human heart. A child's heart."

CASTAWAY

Chişinău, November 2004

It is difficult to think about Eastern Europe and the former Soviet Union without metaphor, which has, after all, sustained generations of writers and poets wrestling with an often contradictory and problematic reality. Romanian-born poet Andrei Codrescu captured this dependence succinctly when he wrote, "*Si fara metafora nici nu pot spune ce ma obsedeaza— without metaphor I cannot say what obsesses me.*"

Perhaps that reliance on metaphor is a reflection of a history of cultural molestation, invasion, occupation, subjugation, and upheaval. Or maybe it is a legacy of a political reality in which the truth could only be approached obliquely. Much of Kafka's work, like *The Trial, The Castle,* and *In The Penal Colony,* were more than just absurd, grotesque, and terrifying: they conveyed the reality of rule by both arbitrary terror and indifferent bureaucracy with far greater accuracy than any literal rendition could. Long banned in the Soviet Union, those works probe the relationship between the individual and society, between culture and identity.

In Kafka's "The Metamorphosis," Gregor Samsa awakens to find he has been transformed inexplicably into a giant cockroach. There he is, literally cast out of his own skin, but still possessing all of his inner sensibilities, still in familiar surroundings. How different is this from the misadventures of a minor bureaucrat in Nikolai Gogol's "The Nose," a story in which a man named Kovalev also awakens to a disturbing and dramatic transformation: his nose has simply vanished during the night, taken off on its own for reasons he cannot fathom.

It is not such a stretch to see parallels between Gregor Samsa and Collegiate Assessor Kovalev and hundreds of millions of souls in the former constituent republics that comprised the Soviet Union. They awoke one day in 1991 to find their identities and circumstances profoundly altered, for better and for worse. No longer were they citizens of one of the world's two superpowers. For republics with long-suppressed national aspirations, like Ukraine, Estonia, Latvia, and Lithuania, it was liberation, but those republics whose borders and demographics were created out of Soviet imperial expediency, the reality was very different. In Moldova, the situation is particularly interesting: there is no history of formal nationhood here, no possibility of union with neighboring Romania, with whom it shares a common language and culture, and which has long been indifferent to its progeny east of the Prut River. Yet with an ethnic Romanian majority of about 66 percent, annexation by Ukraine or Russia is also out of the question. Furthermore, numerous opinion polls indicate that the ethnic majority in what was formerly the Moldavian Socialist Soviet Republic overwhelmingly oppose reunion with Romania, under whose rule they also suffered, albeit briefly.

So here they sit, orphaned by history and independent, at least in name, because no other options exist. With their eyes and most of their hearts turned towards the West and the European Union, they remain tethered economically to the East, especially to Russia. Among its first acts as a new nation in 1991 was the passage of a law declaring Romanian the state language—an impulsive but understandable signal to the approximately 26 percent of the population who were ethnic Russians and Ukrainians. It was, however modestly, payback for a half-century of what many regarded as a Russian occupation bent on destroying their indigenous culture. For the ethnic Russians, long accustomed to being masters of the house wherever they were in the Soviet Union, that language declaration was a rude stick in the eye, a provocation.

As in Moldova, millions of ethnic Russians are scattered through-out the former USSR, citizens of countries to which they feel no alle-giance, citizens by circumstance and default. Evghenia Amambaeva is one of those, now technically a Moldovan, guaranteed the rights and privileges of citizenship in Europe's poorest country. She does not mix with her ethnic Romanian countrymen, preferring her own tight network of Russian-speaking friends. Although she has been in Chişinău since she was eight years old, in 1968, she has not learned Romanian, nor does she intend to. The idea is insulting to her, as is the notion that Russians should be unwelcome or that she is somehow an occupier.

"My father was assigned here in 1968, and we all moved here from Leningrad," she says. "It was normal: he was a colonel in the army and was reassigned to another part of the country. How could we be occupiers in our own country? Russian was the official language of the Soviet Union, and we have done nothing wrong in coming here. Now I should learn this stupid language? I will not!" She angrily stubs out another Monte Cristo Light in the now nearly full ashtray that was empty when we arrived.

The harsh, brittle tone of her voice surprises me as she vents in carefully articulated English, which she studied for eight years as a student. I am also again surprised by her arrogance, something that is not uncommon among Russians. But neither the harshness nor that attitude seems to go with the gentle face sitting across from me. At forty, Evghenia is still very attractive in a typically Russian way: her high cheekbones and very slightly slanted gray eyes have a hint of the Asian steppes in them, her light-olive skin remains clear and smooth, and although her blond hair is beginning to show a few strands of gray, she has so far avoided settling into the matronly plumpness so common among Russian women her age. Tonight she is dressed somewhat formally, having just come from work, looking elegant in a dark skirt, lace blouse, vest, and high-heels. She would not be at all out of place in a New York or Parisian corporate office. She smells faintly of citrus and strongly of cigarettes.

I have known Evghenia for three years and we generally get together for supper once during my annual seminars in Chişinău. She is one of my only ethnic-Russian contacts in Chişinău and the only journalist I know working exclusively in the Russian-language press, which still dominates the capital. She mostly produces short, gauzy profiles of various business people in the city. I have met her daughter, Larissa, who is at the university now, and her ten-year-old son, Daniel, but I have never been invited to their home, nor have I met her parents. She is divorced from her husband, who was a dissident during the Soviet period, and says she has absolutely no interest in either dating or being in another relationship. "My work and my family are enough," she has told me. "My marriage was very, very difficult for me."

At dinner tonight at a downtown restaurant, we are discussing the huge public outcry over the recently elected Communist government's plan to reverse the 1991 language law and make Russian language instruction mandatory from the second grade in all Moldovan schools. When I ask how she feels about the nearly hysterical reaction to that plan, she emits a short, caustic bark and shakes her head. "I cannot understand it," she says through tight lips. "Without us Russians, Moldova would be nothing. *We* are the ones who drive this economy. *We* are the ones who bring in the money. If it weren't for us, this place would still be a cow pasture. I have every bit as much a right to be here as anyone else. And to speak my own language."

Evghenia's eyes narrow, and again the hard edge has crept into her voice. She reaches for another cigarette, jabs it into her mouth, and lights it. She inhales deeply, then expels the smoke in short, angry bursts. "My father served the Soviet Union. My mother was a teacher here in Chișinău. Now, for their pains, they are both old and sick and living on pensions that are worthless. We would pack up and leave this hopeless excuse for a country in a minute if we could and go back to Russia, our Russia, but there is nothing there for us now. We have been gone for more than thirty years. Thirty years! We built our lives here."

Tears of frustration well up in her eyes, and I wonder if I have been too blunt and persistent in my questions. When I tell her I am sorry, she shakes her head and smiles ruefully. "Don't be sorry. At least you are interested in our side of the story. You don't judge me. This is the way it is, at least for right now, but if I ever get the chance to leave here I will. This is a nice city, and for a long time it was home to me, but now I feel like a castaway, like an exile."

I am always sad after my dinners with Evghenia. I think of her sliding into lonely middle age, miserable in the courtly, lovely capital of this most improbable nation. How strange it must be to struggle for balance, sanity, and identity when the world you have known vanishes almost overnight. In one sense, it is the story of exiles everywhere, but here in the former Soviet Union it is different. Here, as Kafka and Gogol would understand perfectly well, you can take that awful journey to a sad land without moving a single step.

GRAZIE, ITALIA
Chişinău, April 2006

Wednesdays are unofficial holidays in Moldova. Every Wednesday, beginning at about seven o'clock, vans park near the circular and whimsically garish home of the national circus. In the windshields of each are the names of towns: Torino, Bologna, Firenza, Roma, Milano, San Bonifacio, Veniția, and dozens more. Inside these vans are meticulously labeled packages for delivery, packages containing everything from children's shoes, sweaters, hats, and jackets to carpets, pots, pans, coffee makers, and larger items like refrigerators, washing machines, and small motor scooters.

Throughout the day, thousands of Moldovans across the country visit places like this to claim their bounty. In Chişinău alone there are at least eight such locations. Old women in headscarves, young ones in skin-tight jeans and high heels, veterans with a few Soviet medals pinned to their threadbare jackets, and sometimes children gather around these vehicles to claim what was sent from Italy the past Saturday. The vans will begin the return trip later in the day, arriving back in their designated towns in time to pick up another shipment.

It is for the drivers a grueling and sometimes dangerous job, but they are well paid for their efforts, which sometimes involve illegal shipments of hard currency buried in large boxes of clothing or inside appliances. Rarely are there problems crossing the border back into Moldova, however. Arrangements can always be made and the government has so far shown little interest in delaying this weekly arrival upon which many Moldovans depend for survival.

We are here to pick up a package from Nicolae's wife, whom I last saw shortly before she went to Italy, where she has taken care of old people for the last five years. The packages come with less frequency, as does the money. We approach the back door of the van, and Nicolae scans the cargo area. It is crammed with tightly wrapped boxes of all sizes as well as with washing machines, dish washers, and hot water heaters still in their factory crates. The driver nods at Nicolae. "Name?"

"Pojoga, Nicolae."

"Parcel number?" Nicolae hands him a ticket, and a minute later the man returns with a small, carefully wrapped bag.

As we walk away, Nicolae studies the parcel. "It's only some biscuits and a couple of little things, but I will have to hide this until tonight anyway," he tells me, shaking his head slowly. "Otherwise, if Ileana and Anica open this without a United Nations mediator, there will be civil war in the Pojoga household. I am sure of it."

In Moldova, Wednesdays are called *Grazie, Italia*, but beneath the joke lies a bleak statistic: one-third of the nation's eligible workforce are employed outside the county, most of them illegally, most of them women, and most in Italy. For some of these women, the journey ends in the worst possible conditions: hired under false pretenses and sold into sexual slavery.

For the majority, however, the reality is more benign although still difficult. They become nannies, maids, attendants to the elderly, orderlies, but all are illegal and therefore vulnerable to any number of predations. In a county where the official average income is about a dollar a day, where the economy has flat-lined, and where unemployment is chronic, the relatively high pay is worth the considerable risk, but the consequences are far reaching. Many of those women are mothers, their children left behind to be tended most often by grandparents. By some estimates as many as one-third of the children in Moldova are now growing up without mothers, and the effects of this deprivation ripple throughout the entire society.

On average, Moldovans working abroad send home nearly $1 billion a year. As a result, Moldovan currency, the leu, is probably the most stable in Eastern Europe, having moved little against either the dollar, pound, or Euro in the last seven or eight years. While those remittances have enabled families to live far better than they could on meager official salaries, that money has also fueled serious inflation that bears no relationship to prevailing wages that remain the lowest in Europe. Even more important, however, are the emotional and social consequences of what many here call the Italian Syndrome.

For the mothers, the reality of leaving the family is invariably painful, and often the hard decision to migrate is a shared one, reached with difficulty among family members; nevertheless, a Maastricht University Graduate School of Governance survey of migrant Moldovan mothers in Italy notes that emotional support for these young women is often lacking, and they are frequently and stereotypically portrayed as venal and selfish. No matter how considered the decision, however, it is the children who most acutely feel the consequences and who are the least likely to understand.

Last year I went to Chişinău's largest cinema, the Patria, to see the Moldovan premier of *Be Free*, a series of one-minute videos by Moldovan teenagers. These were created during "Video Laboratory," a two-week camp on the Black Sea in Ukraine, part of a UNICEF effort to combat AIDS where it is beginning to occur at alarming rates. While many of these shorts concerned contraception, tobacco, and drugs, some focused on the pain of abandonment.

Three in particular stood out. Daniella Cerguta's *We Need You, Mothers* begins with a close-up of two sisters strolling hand in hand. The scene dissolves into a happier, more domestic moment when the mother, now present, is braiding the hair of the older daughter, who in turn brushes her little sister's hair. The scene is full of laughter and light, but it soon fades to a far darker one with the two sisters alone again, unsmiling. The older one braids her younger sister's hair, but there is no sign of laughter or joy in either of them. This dissolves to a final shot, a fancy doll splayed grotesquely on the floor. Over this is written, "We won't miss cool things sent from Italy...We need you home, Mother."

Oxana Chebonic's one-minute video echoes this yearning. *Wish You Were Here* begins with a teenaged girl alone in her room. She petulantly empties her purse on the floor, lights up a cigarette, and then begins putting on makeup. When she notices a note that had been in the purse and now lies beside it, she picks it up slowly. "I love you and miss you," the note says, and it is signed "Mama." The girl then walks to her window, opens the drapes, and looks out into the distance. It ends as it began, with the words *Wish you were here.*

Tatiana Rosu's *We Should Be Together* begins with a boy of about fourteen sitting on a door stoop looking at a photograph of a smiling, middle-aged woman. Soft piano music plays in the background as he tenderly places it back in his rucksack and begins walking down a crowded street. Then we see a girl writing something on a piece of paper. The camera pulls in to reveal one word: *Mama.* She then folds the paper into a paper airplane. In the next scene the boy and girl bump into each other, meeting each other for the first time. In the collision, he drops a piece of paper, a small map of southern Europe, and she drops the paper plane. He sits with her in the final scene, pointing to the boot of Italy. The clip ends with this image, over which is written *Somewhere there is my mom.*

After each of these short videos, a collective sigh filled the theater, a shared sadness that settled over that darkened, cavernous room.

*   *   *

The village of Cărpineni lies about fifty miles southwest of Chişinău. By the only public transport available, a microbus, it takes just under two hours. Today, it is a long two hours as the driver has somehow crammed nearly thirty of us into a space legal for twelve. Nicolae and I are lucky to have seats, but given the relentless press of bodies, the stale air, and the brutally rough roads, it hardly makes a difference.

The day is cold and windy, unseasonably so for early April. Outside the filthy, streaked window, the relative gloss of Chişinău—reportedly the greenest city in Eastern Europe—vanishes quickly just beyond the city limits. I think again of what Tudor Petrov told me in 1998 when he referred to it as a large Potemkin village, and one has only to leave it to understand that the distinctly unglossy reality of Moldova lies just beyond the capital.

The city quickly gives way to steeply rolling, scruffy vineyards that I am told now produce wine of only minimal quality, suitable for bottom-end domestic consumption. Other regions such as Cricova and Purcari produce excellent wines suitable for export, but a recent Russian embargo on Moldovan wines has crippled what little export potential the country has. This is only the latest in Russian President Vladimir Putin's exercise of "soft power" to force the Moldovans to settle the Transnistrian crisis on terms favorable to Moscow. To citizens of this already crippled nation, "soft power" is a deceptive term; there is nothing soft about economic ruin and hunger. Equally unfortunate is the protectionist posture of Western Europe, which has effectively shut out exports of relatively cheaper Moldovan wines, fruits, and cheeses.

We pass a curious relic of Soviet times on our left, the shell of a thirty-story tower in the middle of an empty field. "This is a *very* interesting artifact," says Nicolae. "This structure, according to our brilliant Soviet planners, was to be the greatest wine research institute in the world. It would house experts from all of the wine-producing regions of the Soviet Union— Moldova, Georgia, Armenia, and Ukraine—in a modern skyscraper. Soviet wines would rule the world." He shrugs. "Of course, they were delusional."

Construction stopped immediately upon the demise of the Soviet Union in 1991, and, Nicolae explains, no money exists either to finish or remove this intrusive monstrosity. So it stands, ugly, phallic, and useless in a field where cattle graze nearby, oblivious to the looming intruder.

"Really, it's just another metaphor for the vanity of empire, I think," Nicolae says, and he is right. The crumbling remains of Soviet agriculture litter this countryside, which is full of compounds of huge cement barns with collapsed roofs and rusting metal silos and dumps full of long-defunct Belarus tractors, Don combines and Kamaz trucks. Where there was once sustainable dairy and wine industries, only these blighted legacies remain.

The bus rattles, groans, and shakes its way through Hîncești, eventually turning off the main road at a sign for Cărpineni. It will take us more than thirty minutes to cover the remaining nine miles, all of it over a shredded ribbon of hard-pack clay, deep potholes, and vicious washboard. Any trip through the Moldovan countryside will illustrate one of many interesting points about Soviet infrastructure: although considerably larger than the United States, the former Soviet Union had a network of roads about one-fifth the size of that of the US, and since 1991, in Moldova, that infrastructure has seen little repair and an exponential increase in traffic. The results have been predictably unpleasant.

Cărpineni is unusually large for a village, or rather it used to be. During Soviet times it was developed as part of a huge model collective farm specializing in wine making, fruit canning, and dairy. There was no unemployment, at least not officially, and the land was worked intensively if not efficiently. Moldova, then the Moldavian SSR, was essentially a colony, exporting nearly all of its agriculture produce to the rest of the Soviet Union, and very little remained to grace the local tables. In the exhaustively researched *From Moldavia to Moldova: the Soviet-Romanian Territorial Dispute*, Professor Nicholas Dima notes that during the 1970s and 1980s, 92 percent of canned food was sent to other parts of the Soviet Union, as were 70 percent of its wine, nearly 90 percent of its brandy and tobacco, and almost all of its fresh fruits and vegetables.

Approaching the village now, I see little evidence of any kind of agriculture beyond the home gardens and some narrow strips of private plots that have been recently plowed. Most of the fields appear fallow, scruffy pasture now for the few scrawny horses and cows that graze the treeless landscape. Broken beer bottles, plastic soda containers, cans, discarded paper, and cardboard boxes litter the roadside and fields. "My God, just look at this mess," Nicolae says, pointing to the trash.

Traffic thins to a trickle as we get farther from the main road. We rattle past horse carts hauling rough lumber, hay, and concrete blocks, and they seem far more appropriate given the road conditions than our groaning Mercedes microbus.

The bus deposits us in front of a dim, smoky bar and then groans on towards the next town as it spews oily exhaust in our faces. Inside, men glare at us suspiciously from behind bottles of Chișinău beer and plumes of cigarette smoke. There are no women. Russian rapper MD&C Pavlov's "Dance in Extazy" blares from a tinny set of speakers behind the bar. Nicolae asks for directions to the kindergarten, where we are expected. One man wearing an oily toque points behind him. "Up the road," he grunts before returning to his beer.

The cold, damp wind blasts our faces with fine road sand as we walk the half-mile to the school. Across the street we pass the police station, which occupies the bottom floor of a building with boarded-up windows on the second story. Other buildings are in similar condition, two-story unpainted concrete block structures with ribbed asbestos roofs and smashed-out glass. The streets are largely empty, and we see mostly old men and babushkas. Staring at the deeply rutted muddy streets, the mean, squat ugliness of the buildings, and the ubiquitous trash, I think of the very different *Soviet Life* depictions of quaint and thriving villages that so captivated me as a child.

Nicolae stares at the two Lada police cars parked on the sidewalk outside the police station. "I think Moldovan villages have become very unpleasant places," he says.

"So, was the mighty collective all a myth, another Potemkin?" I ask, inclined to agree with him, at least as far as Cărpineni is concerned.

"In some ways, sure. Remember we couldn't even grow enough grain to feed ourselves, even with Ukraine, a colossal, unimaginable stupidity. But you would never have seen filth like this in the Soviet period, or before. Never. This is a modern disease."

Peeling paint, decaying stairs, cracking concrete, and broken windows at what was obviously a much larger kindergarten facility during Soviet times suggest years of atrophy and neglect. In one corner, however, there are signs of life: crisp lace curtains grace windows of the wing farthest to the right. Here the stairs are intact, and we enter.

Inside, we are greeted by teachers Iulia Lazard and Vera Vasilie, and school cook Zena Leonti, all in their middle forties. It is cold in this room, and they are clad in heavy sweaters over cotton print dresses and nearly iridescent, intricately patterned headscarves of black, gold, orange, yellow, red,and blue. These women seem timeless and stolid; I find them beautifully comforting.

In another room, about thirty children sleep, each in a tiny, snug bed. A small coal stove chugs away in the center; the curtains are drawn over the large, drafty windows, and so in here it is pleasantly warm. In the adjacent room we sip hot, sweet tea seated at a table made for little children, knees practically tucked beneath our chins. To conserve precious coal, this room is not heated today; the large combination coal/wood cook stove in the corner is cold.

"This is the only reliable routine most of these children have," says Iulia, her pale blue eyes angry, her narrow face gaunt. "We have only a fraction of the children we did before the village started dying, and now we are down to eighty, and sixty of those have no mothers here. They have left, most for Italy. In some cases, both parents have left. Many of these little ones do not even remember their mothers, who left when they were maybe a month old."

Zena nods slowly, her hands clasped tightly in her lap. "It's true, and, of course, terribly sad. You ask some of these children their mothers' names, and they will tell you, 'My mother's name is Grandma.'" She shrugs and sighs deeply. It is, I think, a fatalistic exhalation in a minor key, the essence of a people who have endured centuries of violation and calamity. I can imagine tens of thousands of such sighs when Stalin forced collectivization upon these women's parents, and when half a million of their compatriots died of famine and bureaucratic idiocy in 1947.

"Obviously this was a much bigger school before," Iulia says, tilting her head toward the decaying wings of the school compound. "Ten years ago, we had twelve thousand of us living in this village. Now about four thousand are left. Five thousand have gone out of the country to work—most in Italy."

"And the rest?" I ask, wondering about the other three thousand.

Iulia shrugs. "The old people have died, most of them." And most of the young have left because they had to, she insists. "Our young women leave mostly because they are the most likely to find work in Europe, not the men. Thousands of jobs are there for those willing to work as household maids, cooks, nannies, and attendants for the old and infirm. Maybe in Chişinău, it is different. I am sure some women leave simply to escape the misery of their lives, not because there are no alternatives, or because they want the adventure or more money or something they cannot find in Moldova. But here, you've seen the conditions. There *is* no work for our women, and the men have no prospects either. Where is the money going to come from?"

The reality of going to Italy is a daunting one, the problems beginning before the journey itself. "It is very dangerous from the moment you decide to go," explains Vera. "It costs as much as thirty-five hundred Euro to set this up, and then there is no guarantee it will work. That money is borrowed, and it has to be paid back. A woman who was my neighbor has three kids, the oldest is nine. She is now in prison in Hungary because they arrested her at the Austrian border. The gangsters who were taking her to Italy left her to fend for herself, took her money, and abandoned her on the wrong side of the border. There is only *one* way now she can repay that money she borrowed. If she returns here, her husband will beat her, maybe even kill her, and she will have no chance to work anyway."

"What will she do?" I ask.

Vera grunts. "Go to Turkey and sell herself probably. What other choice does she have now? She is still young and pretty, under thirty. But once that happens, there is no coming back here. The road home is closed. And she is not the only one. This happens all the time, and our government pays no attention to this tragedy.

"But most, of course, get safely to Italy. Many mothers in this village send good money home, but that creates problems too. The kids spend it on stupid things like cell phones and then later cigarettes and then in the bars. What else will they do with it? There is no way for them to earn money here, only spend it. For the kids with mothers in Italy, they see their future there, not here. The effect is a bad one, and it is corrupting the morality of our children. It is the phenomenon of kids without parents here."

Iulia nods emphatically. "From every aspect, it is a tragedy here, it is a tragedy for a child to grow up without her mother. At least for the little ones who come to the kindergarten, we provide some safety for them; we feed them three times a day and can see if there are any health problems. We make sure they get their immunization shots. But for the ones who do not come here, it is much worse. Some kids have never really met their mothers, at least since they were one month old, and we call them 'new orphans.'"

When the women do return to visit, a risky prospect in itself, the results are often bad. In the past five years, Nicolae's wife Floarea, who had sought work in Milan, has returned only once, a visit precipitated by the death of her own mother and Nicolae's increasingly desperate pleas for her to come home to her children. Her brief return, however, ultimately did little but propel the family into a deeper cycle of despair.

I saw Floarea twice during this period, once during one of my week-long seminars at the Independent Journalism Center in Chișinău. During a supper that Nicolae cooked, she refused to join the family at the table. Instead, she began taking down suitcases from above a large wardrobe in the hallway. It was a disturbing and bizarre moment during which she was, for all practical purposes, simply gone away to a place somewhere deep inside of herself, to her own Italy.

Systematically, she opened each of the empty suitcases and sighed loudly. She stared inside, slowly running her hands around the interior fabric. There were three of them, and she continued to do this throughout supper. She came into the kitchen once, to get a cloth that she dampened with water. Nicolae, Ileana, Anica, and I sat at the table while she repeatedly wiped down the suitcases, less than ten feet away from us. She might as well have been in Torino.

"She has gone mad," Nicolae said softly. "What else can I think? She will not talk about any of this, but look at her. She is telling us *something.*"

Nicolae's story is, unfortunately, a common one. Rarely are these visits without complications. "Many times the women when they come back will not sleep with their husbands. They declare they no longer love them," says Vera. "Of course, it's understandable. Often they have new loves. You see, our men are not so beautiful."

Zena begins to cackle. "Oh, I love that one: *not so beautiful.*"

"Well, it's true," says Vera. "They have problems with their teeth, they are not very polite, not very romantic."

I glance at Nicolae, but he seems unaffected by Vera's comments.

Vera's voice grows louder. "They don't buy flowers, and often they are beating their wives. Now the Italian men, they are sweeter. Sometimes the mothers are able to take their children to Italy, and that is considered the best ending, the *only* happy ending, but not for the men. The mothers leave their husbands here to die. Most of the mothers leave their children with their parents because they know that the men cannot properly care for them. Once that happens, what is left for them?"

"You think all Moldovan men are like this?" I ask.

Vera wraps her shawl tighter around her shoulders and shakes her head. "Of course not. No, not all of them," she says, retreating slightly. "I know there are exceptions."

And I know that during Floarea's absence, Nicolae has assumed total responsibility for bringing up his daughters. That has meant being mother and father, often while holding down three jobs. For the last five years he has cooked, cleaned, nurtured, and comforted. There is little money for babysitters. When he can, he finds time for maybe five hours of sleep a night.

During the first few years, I was particularly worried about him. He began to slip into a state of chronic exhaustion and developed problems with blood pressure, irregular heartbeat, and depression. "I cannot stop," he wrote me about a year after Floarea left. "And I do not know how I can go on either. Some days I am sure I am dying, and I need help here, and the little terrorists, especially Anica, need their mother. I need to sleep but I cannot."

Vera's mouth compresses into a thin, rueful line, her voice softening. "Most of these men will die by the time they are sixty—from liver diseases, lung cancer, or malnutrition. Maybe they pick up some temporary work, but nothing steady. There is nothing left here for them. Nothing. They are broken souls. *This* is our reality, the same as everywhere in this country. We are middle-aged women living in abandoned villages with abandoned land, abandoned kids, and abandoned men."

She glances at Iulia and Zena. "I hate to think what will happen here, to these kids, if we didn't continue to do this. Somebody has to help these kids. But what about after us? I can't see us doing this for more than another five years. And then what? Nobody wants jobs like this anymore, not for the pittance they pay us. Between the three of us, we make less than one hundred dollars a month! A month! That is how much value this society places on its young. All of the young people now, they just want to leave—to go to Italy,

Turkey, Spain, Greece. Anywhere but here. And who can blame them? Even the mayor of this village, his wife is in Italy now. They have a very European arrangement: she sleeps there, he sleeps here."

Vera nods. "The social problems are huge and nobody wants to hear about them. It seems now the value of life is low, like shit. Walk around this place with your eyes open and you will plainly see the reality. This is a ghost town, a graveyard. It's like a war here, only *all* the casualties are civilian."

In the other room the children have started to wake. Iulia disappears through the double doors as the little voices grow louder. Zena begins to prepare the afternoon snack: today, as it is most days, it will be bread with soy margarine and sweet tea. "I feed them three times a day," Zena says, filling the cups. "For too many of them, I think it is all they get. Kasha in the morning, bean soup for lunch and then a piece of bread with margarine before they go home. There is no meat, no sausage, nothing like that for them right now." She puts the kettle back down on the propane stove, adjusts her scarf, and sighs deeply.

*   *   *

If you want to know exactly who has left this village and where they have gone, you can ask Simeon Filemon, director of the local *Casa Cultura* (culture house), primary school music teacher, and member of the mayoralty council. A compact man barely five feet tall, with thick square glasses, Simeon considers himself an authority on the Moldovan diaspora, counting himself among the immediate victims. It is between classes at the Stefan Holban Primary School, just across the street from the kindergarten. Nicolae and I are sitting down with him in a bright blue classroom, which, like the kindergarten, is spotless. I wonder if the only clean public places in this village are the schools.

"My former wife is in Italy, near Parma. I'm divorced now for three years," Simeon says, shrugging with a wan smile. "It's a common story here. She has taken another man in Italy, and they have a one-year-old child together even though they are not married. My daughter, who is now eight, is with her mother in Italy. It is better for her to be there, I am sure."

I tell him I am sorry, but he dismisses my comment with a wave of his hand and another sad smile. "Thank you, but I am fine. I have my work, my painting, my sculpture, and my music. I suppose I am a dilettante, but it has its advantages. Many others are not okay. What can you expect when most of the young women leave?"

The mass exodus is but one more catastrophe to hit post-Soviet Moldova according to Simeon, who feels that centuries of tradition and identity are disappearing as more of the working population try to escape any way they can, regardless of those they will have to leave behind.

"Our whole rural culture is being destroyed here," he says. "We have fallen very far very fast. This village was the district center, a marketplace. It was, during the later part of the Soviet times, a profitable collective. We produced a lot of wine here, but now, in this agricultural country, agriculture is almost dead. That was everything, and now it is gone. There is no policy. You can't destroy a system and replace it with nothing, which is exactly what has happened to us here. When they dismantled the collectives, people got their own plots of land, but they did not get the means to farm them. Without *any* lines of credit from banks or the government, without fertilizer, machinery, seed, our land is useless to us. What agriculture we do have takes place in the gardens, subsistence farming in the backyard behind our houses.

"Our traditional values are being destroyed by this tragic migration. Things like respect for the old, fidelity to the family, care for our children. It is all disappearing, just like working the land. We are a people who got our strength from the soil and from the cohesion of our village life. Our diaspora is very serious. Somehow we *must* involve those people who have left in our cultural life, but part of the Italian Syndrome is that they don't want to hear about Moldova once they have gone. It is a tragedy unfolding day by day. Sure, some money from Italy reaches the kids, but for what? For foolish things. That's what. And now there are drugs; I have heard rumors that it is just starting, and unfortunately I believe those rumors. It is very, very bad news for all of us."

Our conversation is interrupted when a procession of fourth graders enters the room. Recess is over, and we must leave. Outside in front of the school, Simeon straddles his own gift from Italy, a small motor bike that arrived by parcel in a van from Parma. "It's not all bad," he says with a soft laugh as he kick-starts the 90-cc blue-and-white Mariner. "I got my Ferrari out of the deal." He waves once and drives off, weaving to avoid the brutal potholes on the dusty village street.

In the schoolyard we chat briefly with Svetlana Grinciuc, a pretty woman with long, dark hair tied up in a bun. She is one of the few young adult women I have seen so far, and she is supervising a group of second and third-grade students sweeping up part of the cement schoolyard. Each child bends over a straw broom, moving piles of sand and seedpods to a collection point. The children work intently as they talk among themselves.

Svetlana points to a very pretty blonde girl in a long bright-red coat, a second grader standing in a small group of other children. "You want to know how the migration affects us here in this village? Her name is Liliana. This year her mother came home from Italy, pregnant by another man, and this girl's father beat her to death in a drunken rage. He then tried to kill himself with a gun, but his aim was bad. He is now a complete invalid awaiting trial. That is *our* story. We all play a part."

The last bus to Chișinău is scheduled to leave at four o'clock. Today, however, it departs at three-forty, just in time for us to see it lurching away in the distance. As we stare out at the dark, lowering sky, a sharp rain begins to fall, and the temperature is dropping.

"I think maybe it will start to snow soon," Nicolae says.

We walk in glum silence for about a mile, to the intersection with the road to Lăpușna, where we stop to wait. We will have to hitch back to Chișinău, a not entirely unpleasant prospect given our ride earlier in the day, but few cars are on this road and traffic is limited mostly to horse carts and the very occasional tractor.

We stand in the rain and wind for nearly an hour before a gasoline tanker pulls over beside us. The driver, Vasilie, is going to Chișinău and for fifty lei—a little less than $5—he will take us along. Inside the cab of the truck, it is snug and warm. "The roads are horrible, deplorable," he mutters as he navigates around the deep potholes and ruts. Nicolae soon drifts off to sleep, stretched out on the carpeted ledge behind the front seat.

About halfway to Chişinău, the road begins to climb a series of switchbacks between steep hemlock-clad ridges. Wedged between two of them is the small, dank village of Rusca, home to Prison No. 7, a maximum-security facility for women. There is no attempt to hide this fact, no cosmetic applications to soften the appearance of the jail. Sitting high up in this truck, I get a much better view of the place than we had on the microbus earlier in the day. A cement wall with barbed wire surrounds a cluster of low-slung barracks flanked by guard towers. Behind these walls, 240 women between the ages of twenty and forty live, a third of whom have been convicted of murder. Others are serving time for rape, aggravated assault, and theft.

As we pass the main gate, Vasilie downshifts. "A very bad place," he says, over the whine of the transmission. "Maybe not for the men guards, of course, but surely for the women. They say the toilets are outside, and there is no hot water at all inside. They starve them in there, too. Many try to escape."

As the truck labors up the serpentine road, I look back at the compound in the side view mirror. Maybe this whole country is a prison, I think.

*   *   *

It is ten o'clock and Nicolae and I sit in his kitchen drinking brandy. He has been largely silent since our return to Chişinău, but the words now tumble out in agitated bursts. "I cannot stop thinking of that horrible story," he says. "My God, it is a tragedy for us. Svetlana was right: it *is* our story. Italy is killing us, killing all of us. It took Floarea away from the kids and me. Ileana is okay, but Anica was only six when Floarea left. She needs her mother all the time."

Nicolae removes his glasses, behind which tears well. "I have had to watch her for the last five years growing up with this very deep pain inside of her, and she tries her best to hide it, but I know. I am a good father to her, but I feel it every time a package from Italy arrives and every time a package doesn't arrive."

Much later, I am lying on the couch in Nicolae's living room waiting for sleep. Stretched out as I am, I face southwest, south towards Constanța on the Romanian Black Sea coast where Ovid spent his miserable last years in exile, and west toward his beloved mother Rome. His *Tristio* is full of the pain of separation, of exclusion from all he loved, the timeless lamentations of the banished, the discarded and the lost. But it was, even then, an old story. Before him, Homer's accounts of epic wanderings and Sophocles' banished and ruined Oedipus gave form to our deepest pain and yearnings. It is a universal affliction, this longing for reunion, and it has served as bitter muse to millennia of writers pondering humanity's terrible, inevitable loneliness. Maybe above all, this is what Homer, Ovid, Du Fu, Dante, Milton and so many others offer us: powerful alchemy rendering our deepest sorrow into metaphorical flesh.

The notion of a Latin culture marooned in Eastern Europe and existing for two thousand years surrounded by hostile Slavs and Magyars is to me itself a story of abandonment and improbable survival. The historical explanation, of course, is simple enough: Roman emperor Trajan invaded the region that now comprises parts of modern Romania and Moldova, eventually establishing the province of Dacia. For the next two centuries Romans intermixed with the local Thraco-Getians, making Latin the dominant language. Along with it came Roman culture and religion.

The Romans, however, eventually concluded that Dacia was militarily too vulnerable to barbarian attack and abandoned the province, leaving its denizens to fend for themselves as successive waves of invaders raped and pillaged their way across their lands to richer plunder. Despite all of this, and eventual colonization by the Slavs, the Latin identity persisted, Rome's bastard child adrift in a Slavic sea.

And so I return to this metaphor, because it is the only way I can even approximate the emotional truth of the situation here on the tattered edges of ruined empire. There is about this part of the world a melancholy particular to the dispossessed: shipwrecked by history's cruel circumstance, Moldova, too, is a bastard child long abused by its indifferent Romanian mother and cruel Russian father. Neither offers sanctuary, and so millions exist uneasily suspended between two cultures while exiled from both.

Abandonment begets the same, and I see it through history's pellucid prism: Rome abandons Dacia, whose modern day descendants speak the Romance language closest to Latin but who now scorn their Moldovan cousins so recently cut loose by the Soviet Union's collapse. This implosion of empire, this reverse Big Bang, is *the* determining factor for so much of what now happens on the eastern fringes of Europe and beyond. Surely, the economic, social, and psychic dislocation in its wake helps to explain the hundreds of thousands of children living without their mothers, whose ancestral rulers so long ago turned their faces back to the West and left these women's ancestors to their own harsh fate. It is grotesquely ironic, this new diaspora that casts such a web of sorrow and longing across the width of Europe.

I think of the layers of an onion and Russian *matryoshka* dolls— those intricately painted wood figurines within figurines—to help tell this story. But the dolls are too cheerful, and onions evoke images of the domes in the Kremlin fortress, seat of an empire that tyrannized this land for so long. I think too of the salmon's difficult journey from the ocean to spawn upstream in the rivers of their birth, guided by mysterious, vestigial memory, and I wonder if that helps somehow to explain these vans that appear every Wednesday outside of the children's circus on the outskirts of Chişinău or the graceless, dying villages where the land lies fallow.

And I wonder if it explains Anica's constant sorrow. She goes to sleep every night with the portable phone tucked beneath her pillow, waiting for a call from Italy.

POSTSCRIPT
Tiraspol, 2015

In the Pridnestrovian Moldavian Republic, it is a time of celebration. This year marks the 25th anniversary of its improbable, defiant existence, with banners and billboards throughout the country proclaiming that landmark despite its continued unrecognized status. It is also the 70th anniversary of the end of what the Soviet Union called The Great Patriotic War, the defeat of Germany and the reclamation of a vast amount of Soviet territory from the invading Nazi armies. That victory came at a terrible cost with Soviet dead estimated at twenty-five million, counting both civilian and military casualties. As in some other parts of the former Soviet empire, giant billboards throughout Pridnestrovie—the Russian name for the PMR—proclaim this anniversary of victory, but across the Dniester in Moldova proper few such displays of retro patriotism are evident: for the ethnic Romanian majority in Moldova, the end of that war marks for them not liberation but the beginning of forty-seven years of Soviet occupation and cultural assault.

June has arrived, the first bloom of summer, and on the tree-lined streets of this now-tranquil city of approximately 135,000, young mothers push prams—many of their men are away in Moscow working—sidewalk cafes are bustling, and a sweet calm belies the sometimes hysterical news stories in the West about more immanent Russian incursions into nearby Ukraine. Compared to what it was even a dozen years ago, Tiraspol is a city transformed. Significant Russian investment is obvious in the proliferation of new construction, much of which appears to be banks, and in the colorful restoration of many of the graceful old nineteenth-century buildings that line clean, shaded streets.

Gone is the odious regime of Igor Smirnov. In 2011, Yevgeny Shevchuk defeated him in what was widely regarded as a free and fair three-way presidential election. Leading a government of relative transparency, Shevchuk has said repeatedly that incorporation into the Russian federation is "inevitable." A 2006 referendum widely discredited in the West established that the overwhelming majority of those citizens voting (more than 70 percent of the population) expressed an unambiguous desire to become part of Russia, preferring it even to international recognition of the PMR or (a very distant third) rejoining Moldova as an autonomous region. Russia, however, has given no acknowledgment that it is prepared to absorb this noncontiguous sliver of land that nevertheless remains its protectorate with more than a thousand Russian troops still garrisoned as guarantors of a deeply frozen cease-fire.

The PMR also remains heavily dependent upon dwindling but still substantial Russian largess propping up all sectors of its economy. European and American sanctions, along with steep declines in oil prices, have forced this major oil producer to reduce that support, yet according to the Warsaw-based Center for Eastern Studies, the PMR still earns between $300 and $400 million a year from sales of gas it receives free from Russia. In addition, Moscow pays about $150 million for support of infrastructure and a host of social programs including pensions.

Considering all of this, Moldova proper is arguably worse off, having endured a succession of weak, corrupt governments and parliamentary crises. In 2014, $1 billion went missing from three of the country's major banks. The theft accounted for one-eighth of Moldova's gross domestic product, a very significant loss for Europe's poorest country, a loss that has gone well beyond the economic. Years of failed pro-European governments have eroded public faith in the country's modest steps towards integration with the European Union. In the past eight years, according to both the Centre for European Policy Studies, and the European Council on Foreign Relations, support for EU association has plummeted from 72 percent to 40 percent. Concurrently, support for joining the Moscow-sponsored Eurasian Economic Union, which includes Russia, Armenia, Belarus, Kazakhstan, and Kyrgyzstan, has increased to 44 percent, leaving Moldova a country deeply divided regarding its future orientation—which is exactly what the Kremlin has wanted all along.

Russia continues to play a dominant and increasingly coercive role in the Moldovan economy. It is the primary source of foreign investment and directly or indirectly supplies much of the energy resources upon which Moldova depends. In response to Moldova's signing the free trade agreement with the EU in 2014, Russia has hiked gas prices and imposed painful bans on the import of Moldovan wine and agricultural products. Possibly even more worrying, it has threatened new restrictions on Moldovan migrant workers in Russia. Moldova remains highly dependent upon remittances from its citizens working abroad, with more than half of that money now coming from Russia.

On a quiet shade-dappled pedestrian path by the Dniester River, babushkas feed pigeons, men fish off the embankment, and boys whiz by on bikes. I am walking in the late afternoon light, recalling a similar walk with Anatol Philipovitch Platitzyn fifteen years ago. The regime he so reviled is gone, as is he: back to Russia, to Tula, where he died several years ago. I do not know what has become of Ghennady and Natalia Sokolov, but I hope they were among the two thousand Russian troops repatriated over the years. I don't know where Oleg Serov, the young television journalist I encountered in 2000, has landed, but I imagine he has found a better life in Russia.

For sure, much has changed here for the better in a quarter-century of quazi-statehood, but on another level, much has not. Most people in the PMR appear to want to be absorbed into Russia, yet that seems, for the foreseeable future anyway, unlikely. Moldova's dreams of European integration and Transnistria's return seem equally unattainable. Neither is likely to get what is wanted most. It is also clear that whatever ultimately happens will not happen until the Kremlin wishes it so. Until then, as has been the case since 1992, the situation remains frozen, deeply frozen.

"Look around you," said Anatol Philipovitch a long time ago. "You've seen something of this place and of Moldova. These aren't countries. These are amputated limbs."

I think too of my friend Nicolae Pojoga's lament after our conversation with some students at the university here as Platitzyn lay passed out in his car during that unforgettable week in the first year of the new millennium: "On both sides of this river we're waiting for something else to happen—from Putin, from America, from Europe, from God himself. This is a demented farce. We lost the USSR; then we lost our brothers. We haven't a past, we haven't a future. I want to scream."

A quarter-century has passed and still they wait on both sides of divide. They wait for clarity, for resolution, and for an elusive future, still frozen after all these years.

CPSIA information can be obtained
at www.ICGtesting.com
Printed in the USA
FSOW01n1522200417
33257FS